We Had Some Laughs

www.transworldbooks.co.uk

We Had Some Laughs

Dan Waddell

BANTAM PRESS

LONDON • TORONTO • SYDNEY • AUCKLAND • JOHANNESBURG

TRANSWORLD PUBLISHERS
61–63 Uxbridge Road, London W5 5SA
www.transworldbooks.co.uk

Transworld is part of the Penguin Random House group of companies
whose addresses can be found at global.penguinrandomhouse.com

First published in Great Britain in 2016 by Bantam Press
an imprint of Transworld Publishers

A CIP catalogue record for this book
is available from the British Library.

ISBN 9780593076026

Typeset in 11.5/15pt Minion by Falcon Oast Graphic Art Ltd.
Printed and bound in Great Britain by Clays Ltd, Bungay, Suffolk.

Penguin Random House is committed to a sustainable
future for our business, our readers and our planet. This book
is made from Forest Stewardship Council® certified paper.

In memory of much missed and loved 'Waddlers':
Bob, Martha, Sid, Derrick and Robbie.

Contents

Acknowledgements   9

Fires in the Sky   13
Rooney   18
Howard the Duck   21
Clever Clogs   23
Raquel Welch   33
The Mighty Sid   34
Nightmares   46
Gravyboatmen   48
A Dad Apart   54
Mayfair Mansions   58
Atari   63
Dwile Flonking   64
Stalagmites and Stalactites   69
The Wild West of Leeds   71
Advice   77
Bedroll Bella   78
Any Port in a Storm   83
The Indoor League   84
Everybody Out!   93
Revie and Rupture   97
Club Xenon   104

The Prince of Dartness 109
Johnny Dangerously 121
Waldorf and Statler 126
'I'm Jack' 134
The First Days of Darts 139
'I've Seen Nothing Like It In Me Life!' 148
Creatures of the Pub 154
Jollees 159
Jossy's Giants 165
Future World Champions 170
Deep Heat 176
Lakeside 179
Fish Curry 186
Edge of Darkness 190
Fatter Belly 195
Embassy Girl 201
Before the Fall 203
The End of Childhood 211
Poisoned Arrows 217
Manningham Mills 228
Into the Sky 230
Sid's Rules OK 235
The Power 242
Voice of the Balls 248
A Bit of Fry and Waddell 253
The Healing Power of Darts 257
The Death of a Patriarch 264
Valhalla 270

Index 275

Acknowledgements

I always knew I'd write about my dad one day, but the idea for this book came on a trip back to Leeds in the early winter of 2014. I met my oldest mate, Jason Shield, and drinking in the Leeds side streets we once slipped down brought Sid back to vivid life. The themes of laughs, loss and nostalgia were developed over several pints and more of bitter, so thanks to Jason and thanks to Leeds for kicking it all off.

I also need to thank two other men who spent their time in the pubs of the North and the bars of the darts – my stepbrother Nick and his mate 'Ard' Dave Rayner, who helped me remember as much as possible of those Lakeside nights through the haze of years, beers and tears. Old mates Glen Freeman, Simon Briggs and Richard Damms were all free with their memories and stories too. It was a pleasure to get back in touch and talk old times with them all. My mate Matt Knight also shared his boozy darts memories.

I was grateful to a number of Sid's old friends, colleagues and acquaintances for helping to shine a light on some of the less well-known episodes of his life and career. Dick Bramley, Phil Coates and Tim Stirk were invaluable in helping me catch a glimpse of his life at Cambridge, while Charles E. Hall shared his eclairs and many hilarious stories of the Gravyboatmen at his house in Scarborough. Geoff Druett was truly illuminating about Sid's tenure at Tyne Tees, as was Don Atkinson, while John Fairley, John Wilford and Graham Ironside all helped bring order to the chaos of the YTV years. Michael Stansfield of Durham University and the great Michael Parkinson were also helpful in putting together a flavour of these times. I'd also like to thank Alan Walker, Massed Behnoud, Dave Lee and Tom Peck.

Television Heaven website (www.televisionheaven.co.uk) featured an invaluable interview with Sid about the Flaxton Boys that was extremely helpful, while Austin Mitchell's memoir about his life in TV, *Calendar Boy*, painted a useful picture of the time and gave some much-needed context.

In the world of darts, PDC press supremo Dave Allen was as helpful as he always is – incredibly so. The great Dave Lanning gave me three hours of his time and enough stories to fill three books. Thanks also to John Lowe, Mike Watterson, Eric Bristow, Nick Hunter, Olly Croft senior and Olly Croft junior, Dick Allix, James Motley, Matt Porter, Phil Lanning, Dave Clark, Alan Hart and Patrick Chaplin for their assistance, while Clive Collins at the BBC sports department provided a generous and crucial service in helping me track down some archive footage. Stephen Fry was kind enough to find time to send me memories of his night of commentary with Sid.

I'd like to thank the stupendous team at Transworld, in particular my editor Doug Young and copy-editor Ailsa Bathgate. I'd also like to thank the wonderful gang at LAW, including my agent Araminta Whitley.

Acknowledgements

Finally, I'd like to thank my family. My mum Lindsey, my sisters Lucy, Charlotte and Emma, and Nick all gave their memories freely and openly. But it would have been impossible without my stepmother Irene, who supplied dates, stories, suggestions of people to speak to, and a keen eye on the text. Then, of course, there's Maya, Dougie, Vinnie and my wife Seema, without whom nothing is possible. Thanks to every single one of you. Sid belonged to us all.

Fires in the Sky

ONE OF MY clearest childhood memories is of the drive to Lynemouth. It felt like travelling back in time.

We would leave the suburban comforts of Pudsey, the West Yorkshire town where we lived, heading for the haven of my grandparents' home. In contrast to the clichéd remembrance of things past, where days were endless and filled with sun, outside it always seemed to be cold and dark as we wound our way to the A1, my head leaning against the window as I watched the orange blur of streetlamps. I might have had a duvet or a pillow to encourage me to sleep. But I looked forward to the trip to Lynemouth for weeks beforehand and built it up so much in my mind that by the time we came to leave I could barely speak or eat. There was no chance of sleep.

Soon we'd be on the A1, and those streetlamps would be replaced by fires in the sky. Power stations, coal mines, the entire city of Middlesbrough, all belching out thrilling gusts of smoke and flames: the North was on fire. We passed Catterick, Scotch Corner, Stokesley, Darlington – prosaic places that were as thrilling to me as any exotic location on the map. By the time we reached the Tyne Tunnel, I would be barely able to contain myself. Two hours previously I had been in my bedroom. Now we were travelling under a river. Beyond it lay Newcastle, the promised land, and twenty miles further north, Lynemouth.

The A19 is no different to many other twisting, winding roads, but for us it was charged with excitement. By now it seemed as if the whole sky was ablaze. I would count down the roundabouts, the road signs, until the time came to take the right turn that led into Lynemouth. Another roundabout, past the vast Alcan works – more fire in the sky – through darkness and open land until the first streetlamp flickered into view.

The first landmark was the Welfare, a windswept patch of dog-shit-strewn greenbelt. Sid took my stepmother Irene there on her first visit to Lynemouth after a night in the pub. It was the place where my granddad had trained him to be a sprinter, and he was telling Irene stories as they walked on the muddy ground. Suddenly, he dropped into his starting position to show her how dynamic he was out of the blocks. After calling 'Ready, Set, Go', he rose into a wobbling sprint and pelted head-first into an unseen cricket roller. With blood spurting from his head wound, they went back to my grandparents' house to clean him up and assess the damage. As they walked in, my grandma took one look at my dad's bloodied face and assumed he had been in a fight. Her face crumpled with rage.

'Who did that, Sid?' she demanded. 'Who bloody did it?! Tell us, and I'll go and throw a brick through their window.'

Once at the Welfare, we would swing right on to Bridge Road. To our left, the lights of the only pub in the village spilled across the street. A gigantic mock-Tudor building, it was called the Lynemouth Hotel but known universally as the 'Hotel'. In a broad Geordie accent, this was pronounced 'Hot-ell'. As a kid, I always thought it was called the 'Hot L' and wondered for hours about what the L might stand for: Lynemouth? Liquid? Love?

Once, though I'm sure it happened more often, the car stopped and my dad jumped out and went straight in for a pint. Even if we reached my grandparents' house, it wouldn't be long before he and Irene would be taking Martha, my grandmother, for a few neat gins, while I stayed at home with Bob.

Across the road from the Hot L, which I didn't enter until I was fifteen, was the Miners' Institute. Now that was my kind of place and my granddad's too. Everyone there knew him. The next morning, once Irene and my dad had gone, leaving me for the week, I'd be in there with him. It was a long, uncomfortable walk for Bob, his lungs and heart weakened by years in the pit and even more years of Martha's pies, pease pudding and chain-smoking. We'd stop at the old railway bridge so he could catch his breath, and he'd tip his flat cap back on his head to get some air on his face. Then we'd cross the road to the 'Tute'.

As befitting a social club for working and retired miners, the Tute was a spartan place. Three rooms, a bar, an upstairs that held many mysteries, and four gleaming full-sized snooker tables – the reason we were there. My grandfather had been a good billiards player, and I showed an early interest in snooker. Often I was there during the Easter holidays, when the World Championship was on from the Crucible. We'd sit and watch it together on their black and white television ('For those of you watching in black and white, the pink is next to the green . . .'). Because of this, my grandfather took it upon himself to teach me how to play snooker: the importance of a strong bridge, staying low over the cue, a smooth pull back and release, and the importance of not hitting the balls too hard. The last lesson I failed to learn – 'You have the touch of a Nubian midwife,' Sid once said about my impetuosity on the baize – but while I never made it to the Crucible, I do have my grandfather to thank for my mercurial talent at pool.

The walk to the Tute is one I can still make in my head now. When my first wife died in 2005, and I was a single parent wracked with grief and panic and doubt in the dead of night as my son slept softly in another room, I would calm myself by closing my eyes and making that walk. Across Dalton Avenue, through the ginnel, past the doctor's, the chapel, across the road to the bridge, a short pause, then on to the Tute.

As the car passed the Hot L and the Tute, the road veered to the left. Then came a sharp right turn at the garage where my auntie Gladys worked, which was flanked by a small parade of shops: the Chinese takeaway, from where my dad, on his way back from the Hot L, would occasionally buy us supper – 'What have you got?' I'd ask, as my granddad turned his nose up at the presence of 'foreign muck' in his house. Without fail my dad would break into a chorus of 'They tried to sell us egg foo yung' to the tune of Nat King Cole's 'They Tried To Tell Us We're Too Young', starting Martha's infectious, smoky, rumbling laugh; the butcher's, where Martha bought Bob the best fillet steak, purely on health grounds; the Co-op, which seemed to sell anything and everything, though not, funnily enough, the bubble for a spirit level that my uncle Derrick once sent me to buy.

Then, just before the Pakistani shop where Martha sent me to buy her fags when I was deemed old enough – eight, I think

– we turned left on to Dalton Avenue. By now my throat would be so tight and dry from excitement I'd be unable to speak. We would pull up and I'd leap out. The air was so thick with the smoke from a thousand chimneys you could almost taste it. Even now, the merest whiff of coal smoke transports me back to Lynemouth and the days of my youth. At night the air was hazy, smearing the amber glow of the streetlights. I loved it; Sid didn't. He had a weak chest and was mildly asthmatic. A few seconds of the Lynemouth air of his youth and he was a coughing, spluttering mess.

By the time I'd reach the gate and the long path beyond it, my grandfather would be in the doorway. They didn't own a phone, so how he knew what time we were leaving and when to expect us was a mystery. It was as if he recognized the sound of the engine.

Outside, it was always cold; Lynemouth was only a mile or so from the sea, and the nagging east wind that blew in could rattle the bones of the Michelin Man. Inside, in my grand-parents' front room, it was always roasting hot. The fire blazed, lovingly tended all day by Bob and topped up with plentiful free coal that was the reward for his services to the Ellington Colliery. Martha would smother me with nicotine kisses, and a pie or a stew or some broth on the hob would add to the fug. After three hours in a car, I'd always need the toilet, which was a freezing walk across the back yard.

It seemed as if the modern world had ceased to exist.

Rooney

M Y FATHER SID WADDELL died on 11 August 2012, the day after he turned seventy-two. I had been in the North at his bedside for a week before he died. Two days later, I returned to London and my wife Seema, my stepdaughter Maya and my sons, Dougie and Vinnie. My eldest son Dougie had been closest to Sid, particularly since the death of his mum a month before his third birthday, after which my dad and Irene, my stepmother, helped me pick up the pieces. He had known his granddad was ill, and I had told him before I left that Sid would die soon. By the time I got back on that evening of the 14th, Dougie was waiting for me, and we talked and shared some memories of him.

There was a wave of publicity following the announcement of Sid's death, and we all followed it with some disbelief. Seema bought the many newspapers that carried obituaries about him, tabloid and broadsheet, and Dougie, only nine but a good reader, read them and watched some of the tributes on television. He'd always seen my dad as Granddad, not 'Sid Waddell, darts commentator'. He knew he did the darts, and he watched it occasionally, and he was also aware he had gained some fame for the funny things he said, but, as for the rest of us, the reaction his death provoked bewildered him.

That said, Dougie was less impressed with the acres of eulogies in the broadsheets than I was. But one tribute in particular had caught his attention, and he was keen to talk to me about it.

'Why did Wayne Rooney tweet about Granddad?'

Dougie is football mad. He found Rooney's tribute the most impressive by far. 'Sad news to hear about Sid Waddell. Made darts so much better to watch. He will be missed. Legend. RIP Sid.'

'Did he know him?'

'I don't think they ever met,' I replied.

'Then why did he say he was a legend?'

'Granddad was . . .' I stopped.

How could I explain? How do I begin to tell the story of someone born in a tiny pit village in the North-East, the son of a miner, whose brilliant mind allowed him to escape the pit and gain a scholarship to grammar school, who went to Cambridge, wound up in television and, after a series of bizarre episodes, ended up commentating on a new sport that some people didn't consider a sport, forged himself a career by inventing a unique language of commentary, just as that sport which some people didn't think was a real sport took off, and who became a cult hero and finally a real hero to the point that when he died people who liked and loved him did nothing but swap his most quotable pieces of commentary? It's a sequence of events that could never happen again. A story so incredible that if you put it in a novel no one would believe it. Not least because pit villages and scholarships don't exist any more, and the only people who commentate on any sport these days are ex-pros or jobbing journos, not eccentric Geordie scholarship boys with heads filled with books and movies and facts, with minds as nimble as a Derby winner ('or a mind quicker than Lee Van Cleef on the draw', as Sid might have said).

'I'd need to write you a book,' I said eventually.

Howard the Duck

FOLLOWING THE BREAKDOWN of my parents' marriage when I was three, my three elder sisters and I ended up living with my dad and my stepmother Irene. But while I was growing up, I saw little of my dad during the week. He rose early to commute to Manchester and left before I woke, and he often came home after I had gone to bed. As Irene also worked long hours, over the years we were looked after by a combination of child-minders and Irene's mother, Nancy. Sometimes it was left to my oldest sister Lucy or stepbrother Nick to ensure we were fed, if a diet of turkey burgers, crispy pancakes and potato waffles could be called feeding.

However, I occasionally presented a problem. One day with no school, Irene filming and no childminder available, the only option for me was to accompany Sid to the BBC in Manchester. At Leeds station, my dad led me into WHSmith so he could buy a newspaper and a sausage roll, and I was allowed to get something to distract me for the trip over the Pennines.

I selected a comic, he bought it, we boarded the train and set off. My dad buried himself in his newspaper, me in my comic. Instantly, I had a question.

'What is the duck doing to the lady?'

My dad looked over. Howard the Duck, for it was he, was mounting a naked woman with enormous breasts.

'Playing,' my dad said, and confiscated the magazine.

I was four.

Clever Clogs

SID WAS A self-confessed big-head and the source of that cockiness was his upbringing. Though he was born into spit and coal dust, he was lavished with the sort of attention earls and barons would die for. There was no television, telephone, indoor toilet or central heating, but there was, as he would tell it, laughter, love and sacrifice.

My grandfather Bob was one of twelve children. The Waddells were descended from a long line of miners, and he and most of his brothers and cousins went down the pit. He worked at Ellington Colliery, and much of his forty-seven years of service was spent a mile or more beneath the freezing North Sea, first hewing coal and then undertaking the perilous job of drawing down the props and roof supports after the seam had been mined.

Bob worked with Oliver Kilbourn, one of the Pitmen Painters, the first group of artists to accurately depict the cramped, torchlit world of the miner. One of his works is of two drawers in action. One sits, the other kneels, the roof above them inches from their heads, the only light coming from the torch beams on their helmets, while all that protects them from the crushing weight of the North Sea above are the wooden chocks they are bringing down. The claustrophobia is nightmarish. Bob and his mates worked in constant danger of a collapse or a cave-in, of being buried alive or the mercifully swift alternative of being drowned or crushed to death.

Whenever I stayed with Bob as a young boy, I shared a bed with him. Years of early rising and backbreaking labour had ingrained in him the habit of an early night, while my grandmother Martha was a night owl, smoking 'tabs' and watching TV until the wee small hours when she came and slept on a single bed beside us, nicknamed the 'shakey doon'.

There in the dark, while I was pinned under a million bedsheets that felt as heavy as the North Sea, my grandfather told story after story. Usually of his childhood or his treasured childhood Bedlington terrier, Swank, or tales of Sid as a young man. But he never spoke about life down the pit, and I never dared to ask. It was as if he had cast it from his memory: that seam had been mined, and he had drawn down the metaphorical supports.

He was taciturn, with a sense of humour so dry it barely existed. In contrast, Martha was emotional and talkative, with eyes and face wrinkled and creviced from years of smoking and laughing. The Waddells were dour folk from the Scottish Borders, sober and thrifty; Martha's family, the Smiths, were of Irish descent, boozy and gobby. The exception was Mary-Jane, Martha's almost comically stern mother, who smoked a clay pipe and invoked the Lord. I have one memory of her and it's of being splashed with holy water, as if I was unclean.

There is a hilarious family photograph taken on my uncle Derrick's wedding day in the front parlour of Dalton Avenue,

Lynemouth, in front of polished clocks and plates. There's my grandfather, wiry, looking happy; the groom-to-be with a cheeky smile as white as the carnation in his buttonhole; his best man on his knees in front, looking for all the world like a sixties footballer who's just stumbled past. Martha is the centre of the photo in every sense, head turned coquettishly to one side, heavily made-up, pearl necklace hanging low, chuffed as anything that her youngest has found someone sweet yet sane enough to marry. Her hands rest on her oil-anointed golden bollocks himself, a rakish-looking Sid bearing sideburns as voluminous as his overcoat. The whole photograph is suffused with so much joy you can almost smell the bonhomie and booze.

With one exception: to one side, half-turned away from the others, stands Mary-Jane, her grey, wintry presence like those spectral figures that are claimed to be ghosts in the background of old photographs. Her pursed lips could not provide a greater contrast to the broad beams of the others, while her eyes bore into the camera lens. Those viewing the picture are left in no doubt that Mary-Jane believed, wedding day or not, that the devil's work was afoot.

She cast a foreboding shadow over Sid's early life, much of which was spent shuttling back and forth on the thirty-mile bus ride between Ellington, their first home until the move to Lynemouth, and Alnwick, where Mary-Jane's Irish ancestors had settled after fleeing the famine. At Mary-Jane's behest, he went to a convent every Saturday morning to be tutored in the catechism by a formidable nun. It proved to be such a traumatizing and tedious experience that when he was finally released from the shackles of worship he barely set foot in a church again, even if he found Catholic guilt harder to divest.

Mary-Jane had desperately wanted him to enter the priest-hood. My uncle Derrick and I once joked at the World Darts Championship, as my dad danced around wearing only his baggy Y-fronts, pissed as a fart, while the audience hollered with delight, that this ambition had always been unrealistic.

~

All the Waddells I met were cut from a similar cloth to Bob: upright, clean-living and sensible. The Smiths were the opposite, not least Martha's brother Sam, my father's boyhood hero. I have no memories of him, but the stories are legion. He was a broad, strapping soldier who spent four years interned in a Japanese prisoner-of-war camp.

Whether it was his experiences in the war or a natural weakness for the hard stuff, he had a thirst that would make the ocean proud. Sid was always fond of telling the story of how he was struck down by a childhood bout of pneumonia and refused to take his medication, the pills being the size of horse tablets. Martha hit upon the wheeze of asking Sam to pretend to take one, hoping her son would follow. Sam, merry after a lunchtime session at the Lynemouth Social Club, agreed and faked taking a pill. Sid dutifully took his. Five minutes later, Sam fell off his chair and collapsed on the floor. He'd actually swallowed the pill, which had mingled with a bellyful of booze and floored him.

Martha idolized Sam too, which might explain why she never frowned upon drunkenness. Unlike Bob, who would shake his head whenever Derrick or Sid staggered back in from the pub and take to his bed in disgust, Martha would have a roasted chicken ready, which they'd sit on the floor to strip away from its carcass, a far cry from the milk and biscuits I might be allowed for supper at home. Martha liked nothing more than a few hours at the pub, dressed to the nines, necking neat gins; Bob wouldn't be seen dead anywhere near it except on special occasions. Martha smoked a string of tabs, her face permanently enveloped in a fog of smoke. As a boy, I would sit on the sofa beside her as she talked – and how she loved to talk – mesmerized by the growing column of ash at the end of her cig. It would start to droop, and still she did not react, take a drag or tap it. The tension became unbearable: it must fall! But as it started to sag and crumble, she would flick it into an ashtray without even looking or breaking off her sentence. As I recall, her record was one cigarette but only two drags during a particularly heated exchange of gossip with her friend Jean. Once one was stubbed out, she sparked up another.

Bob spoke only when necessary. When he did, it was hard to understand him. He spoke pitmatic, the dialect of the North-Eastern miner. I was twelve before I was able to understand him properly, and that was when he was speaking directly to me. If he was speaking to fellow Geordies, he was incomprehensible. It was a language of its own: 'wor' meant 'our'; 'sharp' meant 'early'; 'clarts' meant 'dirt'; 'hoy' was 'throw'; 'champion' meant 'great'; people didn't arrive, they 'landed'; you didn't go and find someone, you went out 'seeking' them; and everyone, male or female, was called 'man'. 'What the hell ye deein, woman, man?' I once heard him ask my grandmother. Sid briefly nicknamed him Elvis because of how he pronounced 'always'. 'I elvis have steak on a Friday' or 'Wor Sid is elvis takin' the piss.'

Bob read his newspaper, watched the television or tended the vegetables in his garden. Martha went on at least three shopping trips a day, usually to hunt down people to speak to. I stayed behind with Bob. I was more attached to him, talking snooker, sport, anything. But as I grew older, I spent more time with Martha, going with her to church, helping to carry her bags back from the shop, having my hair ruffled by strangers. By the time I was ten or eleven, I'd stay up and watch TV with her, inviting a forlorn, scorned look from my granddad as he went to bed at his usual time.

~

Sid was a prodigy. Martha and Bob, both sharp as tacks but neither of them academically inclined or readers of anything other than newspapers, must have wondered from which planet he had beamed down. Martha said he was able to imitate the sound of a ticking clock when he was six months old. By the age of three, Bob said, he was doing note-perfect impressions of Winston Churchill. 'More ships, more guns, more tatty peelings for Auntie Babs' pigs.' When I knew her, Auntie Babs was a formidable old woman with horn-rimmed glasses and a fondness for handing out biscuits and cracking out farts when she rose from the sofa. She married the delightfully named Jack Snowball.

Sid was reading fluently by the age of four, and his first school report was so good that my grandparents spent half of Bob's weekly wage on a proper scholar's desk, inkwells, lid and all, which made Sid cry with as much delight as a new bike. Thus a pattern was set. Nothing was spared for Wor Sidney Clever

Clogs. Bob took on increasingly onerous and dangerous jobs in the pit for better money, while Martha took on cleaning jobs, all to ensure their gifted son never went without. Their priority, a creed as far as Bob was concerned, was that none of his kids would ever work down the pit. He didn't want them to spend their lives down there in the dark, with its ever-present dangers. To that end, all was sacrificed.

Sid continued to sail through school. The key to his academic prowess was a photographic memory. Whatever he read, he was able to recall. He never lost this skill, and it would play a significant part in his later success as a darts commentator. Almost every book he read, he could recall great swathes of, and he was as voracious a reader as anyone I've ever met. Even though I can't remember seeing a single book in my grandparents' house that wasn't written by Sid, he immersed himself in literature from the time he could read. He read stories of high adventure – H. Rider Haggard, Mark Twain and Robert Louis Stevenson were firm favourites – but also Boy's Own comics such as *The Wizard* and *The Hotspur*. He also buried his head in children's encyclopaedias, reading about Napoleon, Julius Caesar, Boadicea and other historical figures, as well as the mating rituals of butterflies and foreign currencies and stamps. He absorbed information like others drew breath.

At school, all this reading and easy recall meant exams were a cinch. He was asked to sit the Eleven-plus and passed easily, earning a scholarship to the King Edward VI Grammar School. By this time he had a brother, Derrick, smaller, scrawnier but with the same shock of dark-brown curly hair as Martha and Sid. Unlike Sid, Derrick was no bookish swot and never would be. He was mischievous, irresponsible and prone to all manner of mishaps and scrapes. He was funny and as quick-tongued as his older brother but had none of Sid's educational acumen and precociousness. He once briefly ran away from home when he was seven. 'Mum, Dad and Sid are all bigs,' he wrote on his leaving note. On his return, he was chided more for confusing a 'b' with a 'p' than for taking flight.

Derrick was eight years younger than Sid, and it often fell to my dad to keep an eye on him. One time they went to the cinema to watch a science fiction movie. Derrick became scared and started to hide. By the time the film finished, his head was on the floor and his feet were in the air. When the house lights came up it was to reveal that Derrick's curls were glued to the floor with chewing gum. He could only be released when the usherette chopped off a lock of hair with a pair of scissors.

Even worse for Derrick and his chances of growing up outside Sid's capacious shadow, my dad also turned out to be a talented sportsman when he went to the grammar school. He was a fast runner and under my granddad's tutelage became even faster. Sid was brimful of stories of Bob's unique training methods. One involved him eating dried manure, but that could literally have been horseshit. More convincing were the stories of how Bob made him drink homemade protein shakes of raw eggs and milk to bolster his scrawny frame. Bob would arrive home exhausted from the pit, but rather than slump on the sofa, after eating they would go to the Welfare, where my dad would practise start after start. The hard work paid off: Sid won race after race and made the county team, culminating in the All England Schools under-17s 100 yards final in Southampton. He finished fourth but always cursed the rain and wet grass and his fear of slipping, which forced him to freeze in the blocks and denied him his usual dynamic start.

He also excelled on the rugby pitch. King Edward's was a rugby school, and his speed and handling skills soon earned him a place in the first team and then in the county side. But while his athleticism suited rugby, his skinny body didn't. He suffered a broken jaw that meant he could only drink Martha's leek broth for sustenance for seven weeks. I remember as a kid him telling me to put my hand on his jaw as he rolled his mouth; there was a click, the legacy of it colliding with the meaty knee of an opposition forward. The same with the clunk in his shoulder blade that accompanied a roll of the right shoulder: a consequence of a dislocation. There was another grisly story to accompany that injury, told with lip-smacking relish: as he writhed on the floor in pain, his shoulder out of its socket, a doctor ran on to the pitch claiming he knew how to push it back in. Unfortunately, it turned out he was not a doctor, and, Sid would say, face crumpling in recollected agony, 'The daft bastard pushed my shoulder the wrong way!' A broken ankle was the final straw for Martha, who threw his rugby boots on the fire.

Off the sports pitch, Sid was marked down as Oxbridge material when he was fifteen by the new headmaster, himself a Cambridge man. This was sweet music to Martha and Bob, who by now had sacrificed their roomy bungalow in Ellington to move into a smaller colliery house, with free rent and rates, in order to save money to spend on Sid and Derrick's education. It meant the two boys sharing a bed and a much smaller room, and forgoing the luxury of an indoor toilet, but it would all be worth it if neither went down the pit. That was always a possibility for Derrick but not for smart-arse Sid, twice winner of the Clerk to the Governors' Prize for English Verse. Some old school magazines give a hint of his precocity and reveal a few surprises – not least that as a member of the sixth form society 'with the assistance of several slides, [he] gave a talk on French painting in the nineteenth century'. It marks a) my father's one and only disquisition on art and b) the slide machine as the first and last piece of technical equipment he ever mastered.

By the summer of 1958, he had gained four A levels and earned a state scholarship. That autumn he returned for a third year of sixth form at King Edward's, cloistered in a class of his own to prepare for the Cambridge entrance exam (an earlier encounter with some fearsome dons in an interview had put him off Oxford for life), which he passed. He was off to Cambridge to read for a degree in History, swapping the pit head and smoke for St John's College and another world.

Raquel Welch

'**D**AD?'
    'Yes, kid?'

'Who's Raquel Welch?'

I can't remember why I was asking him this. Perhaps I had watched her on TV or seen something on the news or in the newspapers, even though my interest was solely confined to the football pages.

'An actress.' He was sat in the back room of our first house in Pudsey, buried in his book. I think it was *Sharky's Machine* by William Diehl.

'Is she famous?'

'Very,' he replied.

'Why?'

He took a deep breath and put his book face down on his lap. He looked past me, as if deep in thought.

'She . . .' He started to speak but paused. He lifted both his hands in front of his chest, as if cupping two enormous melons. 'She has . . .' He paused again, looking down at his hands . . . 'Arthritis in her hands.'

I was seven years old.

The Mighty Sid

IT BECAME A family joke that whenever Sid was interviewed by a national newspaper, or on radio or TV, his interrogator would always mention the 'little-known fact' – or words to that effect – that he went to Cambridge University. We laughed because it was the one thing Sid always mentioned in every interview, so how it was supposed to be a secret baffled us. It was repeated so often by him and others that there must have been remote tribes as yet unexposed to the Western world who knew Sid Waddell had a Cambridge degree. He even worked a mention into a speech at my sister's wedding.

Cambridge transformed and made him: his bridge between the smoke and coal dust of Lynemouth and the rapidly changing world of late-1950s England. Though he had travelled there before to sit the exam and interview, I often wondered what it was like for him on the day he left: leaving a close-knit home and community where he was the star, with his mates all from a similar background, to go to Cambridge and mix with a group of equally clever men and women, all from very different backgrounds to him, a gauche miner's son with a funny accent. How did it feel to wave goodbye to Bob and Martha at Newcastle station, to watch them disappear into the smoke as the train pulled away and over the Tyne, not knowing what he was letting himself in for? 'You must have been plagued with doubt and anxiety,' I once asked him.

He shrugged. 'Not really, kidda. I was a cocky little sod.'

According to Sid, his only concern was his virginity. Mary-Jane's papal instruction had left him with a sense of fear and guilt about sex. One, it has to be said, he would soon overcome.

I'm not sure I ever believed him about not being intimidated or nervous about leaving for Cambridge. Either the experience was so traumatic he had buried it, or he really was an incorrigible big-head who wasn't fazed by the prospect. The truth probably lay somewhere in the middle. I sense he was somewhat removed from the main thrust of college life, that he never really fitted in. Hence his reluctance, despite his love of songs and skits and gags, to join Footlights, for fear of rubbing up against people that he felt were too clever by half.

He did confess to me that as the train pulled into Cambridge five hours after he had left Newcastle he felt a sense of pure dread. The rain was hammering down, and he had to lug his trunk to the bus stop and ask a conductor where he could get a bus to St John's College, only for the man to sneer and pretend not to understand Sid's thick Geordie accent.

Things got worse on arrival. A porter showed him to his rooms in Chapel Court and told him that he had missed dinner in hall. His mood was lifted by the luxury of his accommodation: he had a shared bathroom, a lounge-cum-study and a kitchen, which was a marked improvement on an outdoor toilet and the double bed he shared with a rowdy ten-year-old. But the silence gave him the creeps, and within ten minutes he was in the pub across the road having a pint, a pork pie and two cold sausages. Thus setting a pattern that endured for his academic life (and beyond).

The pub and the Buttery bar became his second home. He came from a family with little cash to spare, but money was never a problem when he was at Cambridge. His state scholarship was topped up with a Coal Industry Social Welfare Scholarship, as well as various book grants given to him from local colliery funds keen to support the bright and gifted sons and daughters of their members. All his accommodation and most of his meals and other fees were paid for. He once estimated that he had £360 a year to spend on himself, the equivalent of about £7,500 now. Sid managed to burn through most of his stash of cash quickly though. He bought Derrick a record player for one Christmas – on tick. A few weeks later, my grandparents received the bill to settle payment.

～

In his first week at Cambridge, he managed to inveigle his way into the college football team even though he was no soccer player. He was listed on the team sheet as 'Freshman No. 9', because no one had understood what he was saying when he gave his name. But he soon absconded to the rugby team, where his school exploits served him in good stead. His accent still created problems, however. 'Is the freshman centre a German?' one selector was heard to ask.

Being embraced by the rugger buggers offered him entry to a new social life, which helped ease any loneliness or introspection, until a torn hamstring ended his season abruptly. In those games he did play, he is remembered for his speed rather than his bravery. One Johnian teammate, Chris Hoole, recalls a player 'wearing the shortest of pristine white shorts, displaying white legs covered in black hair . . . Sid Waddell, who made most of his runs for St John's College outside the touchline'. This refusal to muddy his shorts might have been related to his reluctance to damage the burgeoning 'James Dean' quiff he was cultivating.

He wasn't to know it then, but his rugby injury would have major consequences for his later career and life. For instead of hanging out constantly with the rugby lads, he found other friends and other places to drink. Sid never ate dessert after gorging on Martha's cream cakes in his early years, which destroyed his teeth, led to a number of crowns and fillings and a lifelong aversion to sugar. So instead of waiting in the dinner hall for jam roly-poly and bread and butter pudding, he'd go in search of a pint and some company in the Buttery bar.

One night in his first term, as he ordered a pint he heard a fruity voice ask, 'Mister Sidney Waddell, would you care to represent the college at darts tonight?' It was Phil Coates, a second-year student who happened to be the captain of the St John's darts team. His selection criteria were arbitrary and haphazardly applied, usually boiling down to who was first in the bar. As Sid was out of action on the rugby field and no stranger to pub sports, the idea of a game of darts, a few pints and a sing-song appealed mightily.

Phil Coates remembers that he had seen Sid throw a mean dart before, so when he walked into the bar and Phil knew his team were a few men down, his selection was a cinch. The match against St Catharine's started across the road at the Mitre at 8 p.m., and St John's emerged narrow winners, with Sid's average arrows a crucial factor. During the next two years, he barely missed a match and was even appointed captain. He invited other friends to make up the team, and when it came to the inter-college four-man teams the core, known as the K8 Killers after their rooms, involving Sid, Dick Bramley, John Champion and John Coombe, stormed to the final in Sid's second year. Practice for the final involved many pints in a pub across the road from St John's, where, according to Tim Stirk, a member of the Killers in Sid's final year, they would play against Kingsley Amis, who was often found in there. Perhaps this was where the Amis family's love of darts was born?

The final provided Sid with one of his most enduring anecdotes. Their opponents were from Selwyn College, which specialized in turning out dedicated vicars. The Killers warmed up with a few pints in the Buttery at six, a rushed dinner in hall, and then got to the venue for 8 p.m. Over more pints they practised hard, their cockiness growing with each sip. They were on their fifth pint of the evening when the opposition arrived: four timid-looking men, one wearing a dog collar. Sid claimed to eavesdrop on their round: three half shandies and a glass of orange. Amateurs, he thought – the Killers would prevail.

It was a double start. Sid missed three shots at double 13. His opponent sparked up a Meerschaum pipe and immediately hit double 20. It had started badly and went downhill from there. Sid and his team were hammered in every sense. The sober tortoises had beaten the pissed-up hares: a life-lesson for all.

∿

Academically, at least initially, Sid struggled with his course in history. This wasn't King Edward VI Grammar School, where he was the cleverest kid in the class. His tutor was Harry Hinsley, an historian and codebreaker who worked at Bletchley Park during the Second World War and played a key role in the campaign to seize and decode the German Enigma machine. This was unbeknown to my dad, but there's no doubt he was intimidated, and it didn't help that he spent more time on the oche than at the books.

Hinsley, my dad said, changed the workings of his mind completely. At first he was critical of Sid's reluctance to trust his own arguments and his tendency to parrot what he read in books. Rather than rely on a collection of facts, he was encouraged to analyse historical problems and provide his own take. Hinsley's cobwebbed study, stacked with piles of books and imbued with the reek of pipe smoke and sherry, was where Sid claimed he learned to think. The historian had a colourful turn of phrase and a way of linking the past with the present. So the French auteur Lamartine was the 'Kingsley Amis of 1848'. This was a revelation to Sid and the basis, so he claimed, of his later commentaries where Ivanhoe, Vlad the Impaler, Emmeline Pankhurst, Elvis Presley and a cast of thousands would have walk-on parts.

But this epiphany was not instant, and in the meantime he waded through an academic quagmire. His cold, lonely room and its books held few attractions in comparison to the boozy warmth of the Mitre, or the craic in the Buttery with the rugby and darts lads. His non-existent culinary skills meant he ate out every lunchtime. He once had exactly the same lunch order for twenty-seven consecutive days: steak pie, beans and a salad sandwich. The college provided dinner and breakfast, and he had a bedder who made sure his room was tidy. In a way, it was no different from being in Lynemouth but with the pub chef and Mrs Biggs deputizing for Martha.

He ended his first year with a disappointing 2:2. But in his second year his studies improved; he followed Hinsley's exhortations to think originally and independently. By now, he was sharing rooms with Dick Bramley and another friend, Alan Walker, which encouraged him to stay in and work rather than head to the pub every night. There was still more than enough of that though, as well as plenty of sport and darts.

Most of his friends were grammar school boys like him, and the women he dated were townies not students. There was also an age divide between him and some of the second- and third-year students, all of whom had done National Service and were therefore older and wiser. Sid missed doing it by ten months – a relief to him. It's difficult to picture him fitting in with the rigidity and discipline of military life, though he would have gone down a storm in the mess.

But according to Dick Bramley and Tim Stirk, who shared some of their memories with me, Sid had no trouble fitting in despite the age difference. Those problems related to class and background that Sid did encounter were almost exclusively with townsfolk. National Service meant that most of his student contemporaries had been thrown together with men from other places and walks of life, and elitism was therefore rare. But Sid's bedder barely understood a word he said, and she was not alone among the locals.

Sid did make some concessions, namely softening his accent to make himself understood. The consequence was that when he returned to Lynemouth during the holidays he was widely pilloried for talking posh. 'Yee sound like yee've got a mouth full of broken glass,' Derrick told him. His accent soon regained its broadness: Dick Bramley remembers a trip to see Sid in Lynemouth when he barely understood a word that passed between Sid and Bob.

In the summer of 1960, Sid indulged his new darting talent in the pubs of the North-East, where he enjoyed another memorable life experience on the oche.

He and his mate Cliff were able to take on all-comers and won most matches until they were challenged by a burly sea-coal collector to a game of 301, double to start. Sid started on double 13 and hit it third dart. Their opponent, with half an eye on the dominoes, missed by miles. Sid's mate hammered the treble 19. Their opponent missed again. After another six darts they only needed double top to win, while the coal man had not started. He stepped up to the oche and paused. 'On a whitewash, eh? Will you give me three in a bed?' he said, meaning: if I can put three darts in the same treble or double, we win the match. Sid and his partner agreed. Nothing up until then suggested he was capable of such a feat.

He stuck each dart in the double 13.

'Good job there was no money on this. You can buy me a pint.'

'Some experiences you just can't buy,' Sid said later. 'It was on that night I sensed the sheer visceral drama of darts: the oche as the Armageddon of the rampant male ego.'

~

Sid lived in digs for his final year of college, though many of his mates were in the year below and still on campus, so he spent most of his time in their rooms or in the pubs. His studies continued to go well, but he made an error he regretted in later life by choosing the Scottish Enlightenment rather than the British in Malaya 1930 to 1955 as the subject of the final part of his modern history tripos, which counted for 25 per cent of his final mark. His choice involved much philosophical debate over the epistemological musings of David Hume and John Millar, rather than the straightforward timelines and rote learning of the Malayan option. In his view, it cost him a First, though he had to admit later that delving into the sociological and historical ideas of Hume, Millar and other enlightened Scots gave him ample understanding of Jocky Wilson at full throttle.

Inevitably, as his time at St John's drew to a boozy close, his thoughts turned to what he might do next. Sid was unsure. He was interviewed for a job with the Trades Union Congress but didn't get it and ended up working in a cardboard factory in Histon, before returning home to Lynemouth to wonder how best to employ his newly honed analytical brain. Before then, Martha and Bob finally made it down to Cambridge to see their son graduate, Sid wearing what appeared to be a dead skunk on his back. The graduation photo, with Sid looking suave and handsome but like he has a nasty smell up his nose, stood well-polished for decades to follow on Martha's sideboard alongside her other, rather more chaste, hero, Mary Magdalene. Our Lady of Sorrows next to Our Sidney of Arrows. Derrick rarely failed to sneer at it. 'It's like a fuckin' shrine,' he'd say.

∼

In the spring of 2015, I went to the archives centre at St John's College. As his son, I was allowed a quick glance at my father's academic file. It held few surprises other than that his hand-writing at nineteen was neat and precise rather than the dead-spider scrawl it became, and that in 1959 my grandfather earned £757 and 12 shillings a year, just shy of £16,000 in today's money. Not a vast amount to raise a family on, but given they lived in a paid-for colliery house it meant it wasn't all muck and nettles for tea.

Of greater surprise was another file. Ever since his departure from St John's in the summer of 1962, a keen eye in the college archives had followed his career. The file begins in July 1962 with the announcement of his degree in the *Northumberland Gazette*, where it was revealed that 'Mr Waddell hopes to do research on the social and economic background to trade union expansion in Northumberland and Durham.' It ends almost exactly fifty years later with a collection of his obituaries. I also found a review of one of my father's darts books in the college magazine and a copy of email correspondence between two archivists in response to a request of his to send some copies of the prelims he sat at Cambridge. In it he is referred to as 'that most distinguished of Johnians, the Mighty Sid'.

It became clear that his career had been as of much interest to them as those of other, more eminent alumni, which is saying something given that the list includes William Wilberforce, Lord Palmerston, William Wordsworth and Mike Brearley.

Even more remarkably, someone had gone through every interview, every burnished anecdote and yarn, extracted the base biographical information and entered it into a timeline of his life. Nothing had been spared: from being a conductor on the buses before he joined university, to his one apocryphal night spent as road manager for the Animals, to the writing, the singing, the producing and the commentating. Every step of his life, each milestone and pitfall and well-spun myth, was faithfully noted down by a St John's archivist.

Afterwards, I walked through New Court, the Gothic 'wedding cake' where Sid had rooms in his second year, and from whose mullioned windows he often puked in the Cam, trying to picture him, whippet-thin, gauche and wiry, walking over the Bridge of Sighs in his gown, green Tyrolean hat with feather, check sports coat, tight twills, black shirt and a pink bouclé tie on his way to sherry with Harry Hinsley, or rushing with his mates to dinner behind the heavy studded oak door of the dining hall. I failed to see it; the place seemed too old, too stuffy, too *grand* for Sid. Yet in the Mitre across the road, now a trap for unsuspecting tourists seeking Ye Olde Pubbe Experience, where steak pies (not salad sandwiches) are still on the menu, I got far more of a sense of him: at the bar sipping a pint, eyeing up a town girl across the pub, absent-mindedly wiping pie juice off his chin, telling a joke, arms and hands whirling and nudging as he wove his tale.

He once told me he did regret not getting the balance right. 'I shoulda been on first-name terms with the lasses at the library and not the barmaids at the Mitre.' Then he might have spent his life in academic seclusion, poring over manuscripts and lecturing earnest students. But, to use a favourite, less academic word of his, he knew that was 'bollocks'. His brain was better applied to less scholarly pursuits and eventually more appreciated for it. And meanwhile, unbeknown to him, his college was not, as he imagined, wrinkling its nose as his career at the more exuberant end of British sporting culture flourished, but revelling and delighting in it, and writing down every detail of his life as if on biblical stone.

It's a shame he never knew. I can't think of any other revelation that would have given him greater pleasure or satisfaction.

Nightmares

I CAN'T REMEMBER WHAT age I was. I can't remember what the dream was about. All I remember is that it was a bad one and that I was screaming. My box bedroom was on the same level as Sid and Irene's. I heard their door open and his footsteps cross the small landing. I continued to scream.

The landing light was on, as I insisted it be. Sid ran in, illuminated in its glow. He was wearing a red T-shirt, nothing else.

'What's up, son?'

I said nothing. He thought it was fear, but the reason I couldn't speak was because his naked swinging knackers were at my head height and two feet from my face.

'It's all right, Dad,' I said.

'You sure?'

I nodded. He went back to bed. I had bad dreams after that, but I never called out again. No nightmare was ever as bad as *that*.

~

We all had similar stories. Naked Sid. Sometimes he would come down in the morning in a dressing gown that was a size too short and smelled a bit of vomit. He would still be half-asleep as he walked in the room while we watched TV, and absent-mindedly he'd undo and do up the dressing-gown belt, giving us an unwelcome, thankfully fleeting, glimpse of his bollocks.

It wasn't just family either. At the darts, my mate Jason ended up sharing a bed with Sid. I must have passed out elsewhere. He was eternally disturbed when Sid got up in the night and walked bottom-half naked to the toilet. Why just the T-shirt? Jason asked me later. Where were his underpants? Why not just sleep entirely nude? I couldn't answer. That was Sid.

Normal rules didn't apply.

Gravyboatmen

O F ALL THE periods of Sid's life, the early 1960s which he spent in Durham remain the biggest mystery. He never wrote about them, rarely spoke of them, and so the details of what he was doing there remain elusive. But it was there his life changed.

After kicking his heels for a few months in Lynemouth, he eventually found a job his degree merited, as research assistant to Ted Allen, Durham University's professor of economics. Perhaps he was still dreaming of that career in the fusty halls of academia? On the surface, the job seemed spectacularly unsuited to Sid and his history degree, until I learned that Allen specialized in the industrial problems in the North of England. He was also a member of the Research Committee of the North-Eastern Industrial and Development Association and had a particular interest in trade unions, which is where Sid came in.

It was his job to supply Allen with figures and statistics about trade union membership, wage movements and levels of unemployment. Meanwhile, he was to write a postgraduate thesis on the history of the Boilermaker's Union (or United

Society of Boilermakers, Blacksmiths, Shipbuilders and Structural Workers to give it its full title in 1963), which as far as I know he never completed (though his research did not go completely wasted: the heroine's father in his one and only novel was a member). The fruits of his research were published in a book, he claimed, though no one has ever seen it or knows the title.

It's difficult not to picture Sid as some Billy Liar figure, trapped in dusty rooms of quiet despair, gazing out of the window, his expectations and dreams being suffocated, daydreaming of a world of liberation, sex and rock 'n' roll, creativity and innovation that he should be part of. Sid always wanted to keep one step ahead of conformity and mediocrity, to do anything to avoid the dull and quotidian, to confound tradition and stuffiness, so it's no surprise that he swiftly grew tired of his life in service to the university.

To sate his appetite for performance and desire to be noticed, he decided to seek out his thrills. Unsurprisingly, most of his time was spent drinking in pubs with students, and one, Charles E. Hall (everyone called him Charles, but until my dad died he referred to him as 'Charles E.', though he rolled it into one so it sounded like he was calling him 'Charlesie'), was musically adept. After seeing him play piano in a pub for half a crown and a couple of pints, Sid decided they should combine talents. This was the era of *That Was the Week That Was* and satirical songs of the week's events, and Sid had an idea they should form a folk duo. Charles E., who was game for any experience, went along with this eccentric Geordie dreamer and so the Gravyboatmen were born.

Their career was chequered. Charles could play the guitar

and Sid could cling to a tune, even if the key was less easy for his partner to detect. But the venues they performed at were working men's clubs and pubs, whose clientele were not particular fans of Willie Rushton and David Frost and were more fond of boozy singalongs than a satirical, sideways take on topical events. (Of course, this wouldn't be the last time Sid's references flew above the heads of his audience.) Neither did the other turns dress in fishermen's smocks and sunglasses like Sid decided the Gravyboatmen should. Occasionally, they had to tailor their act to the audience. At the end of one gig, Charles E. ended up playing musical accompaniment to a stripper whose act involved a python. Who knows where Sid was? In the front row laughing, probably.

Much to Charles E.'s surprise, Sid found them regular gigs. The reception was always lukewarm, but the free beer flowed. Their schtick was for Charles to play a popular song of the day, say 'Diana' by Paul Anka, and Sid would recite his own lyrics to the same melody.

For reasons lost to the mists of time and copious amounts of booze, they were invited to appear on the *Tonight* programme, live on BBC1, and were paid the princely sum of £3 and 3 shillings. It involved driving to Newcastle for a recording. Sid commandeered a Rover belonging to the father of a friend, and Charles drove, stopping off at every pub on the way for some liquid fortification. In Newcastle, they sought more pints of Dutch courage and were more than well lubricated when they arrived at the studio. There they performed a version of 'Blowin' In The Wind'. 'How many roads must a man walk down,' Sid warbled. 'Before he gets holes in his shoes? The answer, my friend, is on the TV, just watch the six o'clock news.'

It is believed that Willie Rushton et al. slept easy that night.

The Gravyboatmen's other career highlight came at the South Bank Sporting Club, a two-thousand-seater venue in Middlesbrough, second on the bill to a Frank Sinatra tribute act. Because of the size of the venue, Charles had to wrap a microphone around his neck to pick up the guitar. A minute into the first song and Charles could tell they were going to bomb. A few claps came from the audience. 'They're clapping us, kidda! We're doing alreet,' Sid said to him. But then came the boos. A few of the crowd rose to their feet, and it wasn't to offer an ovation.

Charles sensed danger. This was not uncommon at a Gravyboatmen gig. One memorable night, someone had thrown a knife, which had stuck in his guitar, but that was in a room with a handful of people, not hundreds all eager for some Sinatra rather than two smart-arses in smocks. He also knew that Sid would not admit defeat, even if that meant a punch-up. He'd been at enough dances and dos with my dad to know that he didn't shy away from trouble. He was no fighter, but he ran as fast as lightning, leaving the less nimble in his wake to take a beating.

'Come on, Sid, let's fuck off,' he urged. But the mic around his neck caused his words to echo around the auditorium. 'Fuck off . . . fuck off . . . fuck off.' A vicious snarl emanated from the audience. They were escorted safely from the building but told to honour Charles's words to the letter and quick.

That was their last gig. Sid returned to the library; Charles's Spanish degree ended, and he went back home to a successful career in North Yorkshire, where one day he would become mayor.

~

Sid continued to daydream. He never stopped writing stories and plays or lyrics. He had read *Billy Liar, Room at the Top, This Sporting Life*; he had seen *Look Back in Anger* and watched *Saturday Night, Sunday Morning*. 'What I'm out for is a good time – all the rest is propaganda.' The lives and struggles of the working class, the people and world he knew so well, were being dramatized, and he wanted to be part of it.

In early 1965, the North Eastern Arts Association held a scriptwriting contest in conjunction with the BBC. The winner's script was to be screened as part of *The Wednesday Play* series, which involved Tony Garnett as a young story editor, on the cusp of fame as the writer of *Cathy Come Home*, and Ken Loach as director. Sid had watched *The Wednesday Play* and admired how its honest portrayal of working-class life and bravery in tackling previously ignored social issues had won it a wide audience. So he entered.

His autobiographical play about a young man from a rough Geordie background making his way at Cambridge finished third. It wasn't made, though to his dying day he remained suspicious that a TV play with a similar theme and story, *Stand Up, Nigel Barton*, written by Dennis Potter, was screened as part of *The Wednesday Play* series later that year.

But as part of his prize he was invited to BBC TV Centre in London for a week, where he shadowed *The Wednesday Play* team. Intoxicated by the experience, and with some supportive words from Tony Garnett, he returned to Durham with a sense of how he might make his mark. Television was a new, vibrant medium, teeming with ideas and desperate for them, staffed with raucous, creative people, a million miles away from stuffy, silent libraries and worthy treatises on trade unions.

A Dad Apart

I CAN'T REMEMBER HOW old I was when I realized my dad wasn't like other dads.

It might have been when I realized that other dads drove cars. Sid never did. His story was that during his fourth lesson in York in the late 1960s, his instructor told him to pull over to the side of the road.

'Mr Waddell,' he said, hands shaking. 'There's no way on earth you should be let loose behind the wheel of a car. Unless it's at Brand's Hatch. Now let's go for a pint.'

Several pints and several hours later, they both agreed his tuition should stop.

His driving instructor had performed an important public service for the safety of the road users of Yorkshire. Sid was temperamentally unsuited to driving. I once saw him get irate with a television that he thought was broken but which in fact he had accidentally switched off, so God knows how he'd have coped with any mechanical malfunction. He once helped me change a flat tyre on my first car, a few weeks after I'd started driving. I was hungover; he was Sid – it took us five hours.

Irene was the driver. Sid was there to map read and light her fags. He was better at the latter than the former. He once advised Irene to make a U-turn on the M1.

His inability to drive gave him freedom, not least to get stuck into the ale. There were few stations in the land where he didn't know a nearby place to snatch a pint. Often he would stop en route. Stalybridge station has a famous bar of which he was fond, and on his way back from Manchester to Leeds he and a few other commuters would get off, sink a few pints, then jump on the train behind.

At King's Cross, there was the bar of the old Great Northern Hotel, which couldn't have been more removed from its current upmarket boutique incarnation. The carpets were sticky and stank, the decor was old and mouldy, the furniture frayed and worn, and the beer never more than average. But Sid, as ever, revelled in the humanity. Squaddies heading back North to barracks, Geordies on the bum running for home, Yorkshiremen celebrating leaving the iniquities and degradations of London behind. One night, in the last days before the hotel's closure, we spent a lost afternoon there playing pool against two strapping South Yorkshiremen. For one of them it was his last day of freedom. He was in court in Doncaster the next day to plead guilty to an offence that carried a mandatory custodial sentence. We didn't ask what that offence was, and we let him and his mate win.

Then there was the Scarbrough Hotel in Leeds, in the sooty 'dark arches' below the station, known universally but for unknown reasons as 'the Taps'. After a few pints in Manchester, and a couple of liveners at Stalybridge, it made an ideal port of call to maintain his blood alcohol level before the bladder-bursting bus journey home to Pudsey. Depending on the time, and how much he'd had, he might even have a last one in the Golden Lion at the top of our road.

It did mean that any journey made with Sid had an epic quality to it. It usually started early, with a boiled egg or a sausage sandwich from a cafe he knew. Then a bus or two, the train, sometimes several trains, and, if we were lucky, the comfort of a taxi.

I was and still am a Liverpool FC supporter. It dates back to when I was a small boy and crossed the path of a football-obsessed, malevolent son of a benevolent childminder. He was a fanatical Leeds United fan, then barely clinging on to the coat-tails of greatness. Liverpool were the new pretenders, and he hated them. In the back yard of South Parade, he would pretend to be Peter Lorimer, with a ferocious shot to match, while four-year-old me defended the garage door doubling as a goal. He told me I was Ray Clemence and would then pepper me from close and long range. It reached the point where I hated Leeds and developed an affinity for poor Clemence and his team, which blossomed into lifelong support.

But living in Leeds I had few opportunities to see my team play other than their visits to Elland Road. Then Sid scored tickets for Man City v Liverpool at Maine Road. It coincided with the school holidays and one of my trips to Lynemouth. So on Friday night Sid travelled to Geordieland, where he slept on the sofa and I slept on two chairs pushed together. The difference was that he'd had several pints in the Hot L to knock him out, while I'd had nothing stronger than a glass of dandelion and burdock, so I barely slept.

We left at dawn, a light rain slicking the roof slates on Dalton Avenue and making them glisten. It was a two-mile bus journey to Ashington, the childhood home of the Charlton brothers Jackie and Bobby. At the bus station, we caught another bus for the long and winding ride to Newcastle.

At the station, our bellies rumbling, we had a second breakfast to top up the tea and toast Bob had made for us before we left. We travelled down to Leeds, where we picked up a rattler across the Pennines to Manchester, arriving in time for a cheese and tomato sandwich. We took another bus to the outskirts and Maine Road, before walking the short distance to the stadium. A man was lying in the road, frothing at the mouth, but people sailed serenely by. I asked my dad what had happened and noticed he was clutching my hand.

'Pissed off he hasn't got a ticket.'

We got to our seats just before the match started, surrounded by a mass of City fans. To my growing disbelief and delight, Liverpool won 5–0, with goals from Lee, Neal, Johnston, Kennedy and Rush. The City fans around us were mutinous. Before the match, Sid had leant in and whispered, 'You're gonna hear some words today that I don't want you to repeat to anyone.' He was right: the air was bluer than City's kit. Sid winked at me with each curse; I smiled.

After the match, we walked for what seemed like hours, then caught a train to Manchester Victoria, another to Bradford, where mercifully we took a taxi. By now it was dark outside, and it felt like we had crossed continents. It turned out the *Match of the Day* cameras had been at Maine Road, but I fell asleep on the sofa before the end of *Dallas*, exhausted but deliriously happy at having shared a magical adventure with my dad.

Mayfair Mansions

Though Sid had spent a week at TV Centre learning how the BBC worked, his first break in television was in the less refined, more rambunctious world of commercial broadcasting. ITV was born in 1954, after much debate among the powers that be about whether exposing the nation's viewers to something as vulgar as adverts might cause the breakdown of society as they knew it.

After a muted, haphazard birth, by the early sixties most regions had a franchise: often one in charge of weekday programming, while another took responsibility for the weekend. The quality was variable: popular quizzes cribbed from the USA interspersed with terribly acted dramas, recorded live with all the mishaps and fluffed lines and cues that entailed, a smattering of sport and a bit of news, often read by stilted presenters with cut-glass accents and little affinity or connection with the region they were serving. Yet there were some successes: notably *The Saint, The Avengers, Armchair Theatre, Oh Boy* and *No Hiding Place*, among others.

By the early sixties, commercial television was also turning a profit and increasingly popular, but it was still coming in for criticism. One perceived fault was a failure to find a regional identity and serve their local viewers. But some franchises developed their own local news programmes and flourished because of it.

Among the most successful was Granada. One of the 'Big Four', they held the weekday franchise that covered the North-West and Yorkshire. Their popular daily magazine show, *Scene at 6.30*, launched the TV careers of Michael Parkinson and Mike Scott.

It was also where Sid got his first TV job, late in 1965, though how he wound up there is something of a mystery. One story is that someone at the BBC was so impressed during his week's internship that they put in a word. Another is that a Granada crew making a documentary about Danny McGarvey and the Boilermakers Union enlisted Sid's help and were so enamoured that they wangled him a job.

Whatever the real story, he gave up his job at the university and took a six-month contract to work as a researcher on *Scene at 6.30*. He rented a flat in the wonderfully named Mayfair Mansions in Didsbury, where he lived during the week, but commuted back to his bedsit on Saddler Street in Durham at weekends to see his mates.

There was another reason for the commute: by this time he had met my mother. Lindsey Holroyd was an eighteen-year-old journalist on the *Durham Advertiser*, a breeding ground for its bigger, sister paper, the *Northern Echo*, edited by Harold Evans. Evans had given Lindsey a job, explaining she was a bit too callow for the *Echo*. So she moved from York, and within a few months, in a pub named the Shakespeare, across the road from Sid's digs, the two met.

Early in the New Year, Lindsey became pregnant, and they married in February. The only two people present were Sid's mate Terry Hopper, a screw at Durham jail, and my mum's mate Marge. Neither set of parents nor their legions of friends were invited.

This secrecy was all because of Sid's Catholic guilt. He had got a girl in the family way and was too cowardly to tell his family for fear of the fire and brimstone that would pour forth from Martha and Mary-Jane in particular. He told Lindsey they wouldn't come as they didn't approve, and to spare his blushes her parents, John, a respectable, avuncular accountant, and Margaret, a warm, generous woman who made a treacle tart so tasty it would make a statue weep, agreed not to come too but gave their blessing. My mum was not aware that Sid had not even told his parents either about the marriage *or* the pregnancy for fear of being cast into the metaphorical fires of hell for his sins.

Little did he know. In 2004, I was the first person to research the Waddell family genealogy. Like all good family historians, I started with the living and asked Sid when my grandparents were married. 'Nineteen thirty-six,' he said with utter certainty. 'Four years before I was born.' I went to the now long-gone Family Records Centre in Islington to wade through the leather-bound indexes of birth, marriage and death certificates. There was no record of my grandparents' marriage in 1936. I searched 1937, 1938 and 1939 with no luck. I tried the years leading up to 1936, but there was still no entry for a Robert Waddell and Martha Smith.

Eventually I found it – in 1940. They had married four months, not four years, before he was born. Martha was a devout Catholic but clearly not that devout. More interesting details were to follow. I knew Martha's birth year and started to search backwards from that to find Mary-Jane's marriage to Samuel Smith. I didn't have to look far. She married him four months before the birth of her oldest daughter.

Mary-Jane and Martha: fallen women. I walked out of the records centre and dialled Pudsey. As always, Sid answered with a booming 'Helllooo!', the first part delivered as he picked up the receiver and the last syllable as it neared his mouth, so his greeting emerged like an oncoming train.

I told him I was at the Family Records Centre. He knew I was rooting through the family tree and told me he always thought his grandmother, Bob's mother, might be Jewish because her middle name was Goldsmith. That turned out to be a myth.

I told him about Martha first. 'Bugger me,' he said. Then I told him about Mary-Jane. The line went completely silent.

I think, in those few speechless seconds, his mind flashed back to Durham 1966, his young bride, their wedding and his pusillanimous refusal to own up to his mum and granny for fear of being disowned. Yet he didn't know his two idols of purity had feet of clay. Neither was in a position to criticize saintly Sid, though, he admitted ruefully, that might not have stopped them.

The first time my mother officially met Martha and Bob was in late 1966, when he arrived at their door with his new wife and their first granddaughter, Lucy. The shock must have been palpable. They didn't even know he was married. But the joy of a baby in the house doused any unrest and quelled any questions.

~

At Granada, surrounded by some of the brightest minds in television, as well as its most exacting egos, Sid's career had seemed to be flourishing. There had been hiccups: notably when Michael Parkinson was reading a script in rehearsal and stopped mid sentence.

'Who wrote this crap?' he asked.

Sid timidly raised his hand and was ordered to perform a hasty rewrite. He soon learned what was acceptable. Parkinson can't remember the incident in question but admits he could be impatient during studio time. He remembers Sid during that period as a lively character with a very good brain. 'Once met it was impossible to forget him.'

Once his six months were up, he was summoned to the editor's office. His colleagues all believed he was going to be promoted. 'What did you get?' he was asked by Barry Cockcroft, whom he would later team up with at Yorkshire Television. 'I got fired,' replied a shell-shocked Sid.

It's never really been clear why. The simple explanation seems to be that his face didn't fit and neither did the stories he brought in. But his first stint in TV had ended in failure. Chastened, he went back to Durham and his heavily pregnant wife, but he was still adamant that his future was in TV.

Atari

THROUGH A LATER job he got working for kids' TV in Manchester, my dad would bring home a steady stream of freebies. Few of these were any good: Keith Chegwin T-shirts, the new Shakin' Stevens single, a signed photo of Modern Romance. But one stood out above all: an Atari Games System.

The day after he brought it home, he and Irene were away filming. Charlotte and I both took advantage of Irene's mum's trusting nature by throwing a sickie. Then we played Frogger all day. For weeks, I did nothing but play Atari.

My favourite game was Decathlon. Ten events, the last of which was the 1,500 metres. Almost four full minutes of furious joystick waggling. At the end of one race, I got up and left the sitting room, red-faced and panting, holding my knackered, cramping wrist just as my dad arrived back from work, a few drinks inside him.

He looked at me and grinned. 'You'll gan blind, son.'

I was nine years old.

Dwile Flonking

AFTER BEING SACKED by Granada, Sid wasn't out of work for very long. Within a couple of weeks, he had secured a job with Tyne Tees on better money, a relief for both him and Lindsey.

If working for the station that served his hometown and his own people sounded enticing, the reality was somewhat different. Tyne Tees might have been based in Newcastle and Sid might have known the area well, but it ran the news programme he was hired to work on in a traditional manner: local news presented in the same solemn, dry style as national news programmes. This serious approach contrasted with much of the station's other output, which consisted of US cop shows and westerns.

But Sid was a geyser of ideas, and he wanted to start in style. Immediately, he turned to a place he knew best for inspiration – the pub. Tyne Tees was lucky to be served by two good boozers: one, the Rose and Crown across the road, while the Egypt Cottage was actually embedded in the building, itself an eccentric warren of narrow corridors and odd-shaped offices that had once been a flour mill.

His idea was to produce a package on pub games like the ones that enthralled him at his local, the Dun Cow in Durham. He and his crew, Ray Jackson on camera and Don Atkinson on sound, started in the Rose and Crown. Don saw boom operator Mike Donnelly having a quiet pint and informed my dad that he was a proponent of Dwile Flonking, which even Sid hadn't heard of. This was a game that involved teams dancing around while one man, the flonker, dips a cloth on a stick, the dwile, in a bucket of beer and then tries to hit the others with it. Sid's eyes lit up as if he'd won the pools: Morris dancing for drunks. He had to film this.

Donnelly was encouraged to round up some of his mates to make up the numbers. For the next two hours, Sid filmed them both dwiling and flonking, making sure their glasses were kept full for continuity. Everyone drank at least six pints of continuity, and it cost him a fortune. He let everyone go, grabbed a few more establishing shots and cutaways, then headed back across the road to cut the film for that night's show, with a couple of records under his arms to play as a soundtrack.

As he walked into the control room, he was almost floored by the smell of alcohol. Slumped in the corner was Mike Donnelly, who should have been operating the boom for that night's show but was now unable to operate his legs. Looking around, Sid could see the addled smiles of a handful of other men who had been flonking and drinking: they were members of the film department, who had taken the opportunity of a free piss-up courtesy of the new young producer with the bottomless pockets. 'You bastards,' said Sid with a wide grin, but already he knew that he was going to fit in better at Tyne Tees than Granada.

~

If his experiences at Granada had made him more pliable and willing to toe the company line, it didn't show at Tyne Tees, where he swiftly developed a reputation for quirky ideas and offbeat stories. Geoff Druett, who went on to become a stalwart presenter of Yorkshire TV's *Calendar* programme but was then a callow vicar's son straight from university, said that in an often po-faced newsroom Sid was a reminder that news and current affairs could be fun. He would fight to get amusing or idiosyncratic stories on to the news list in the face of some hefty opposition. Geoff remembers one story where Sid instructed him and Liz Fox (another future YTV presenter) to bounce around Eldon Square in Newcastle on spacehoppers while jousting with rolled-up copies of the *Evening Chronicle*, which he set to the tune of 'Don't Stop The Carnival' by the Alan Price Set. It's fair to say this kind of item was not common in local news in any region, and nor was it universally popular within the corridors of Tyne Tees.

But that was the way Sid operated: he was an ideas man, and he continued to risk censure by introducing some imagination and razzmatazz to the stuffiness of TV news. It didn't always work, but it was encouraged, or at least endured, by Brian Gibson, his first editor. This occasionally led Sid into trouble, most notably when it came to covering the Durham Miners' Gala.

This event was the highlight of the political and social calendar in the North-East, at a point in history when the Labour movement was at its zenith. Miners, their families and colliery bands from all over the region took to the streets, pubs and clubs, watched over benevolently by members of the Labour government and its leadership. It was a real festival and event, enjoyed by thousands.

But even though Durham *en fête* looked at its best, and the carnival atmosphere swept through the whole area, there was one problem for the local news programme: it made for boring television. Every summer, the gala was covered exactly the same way: footage of marching miners, their bands playing the same tunes; some duly reverent shots of Harold Wilson and his cohorts; and comprehensive, deferential coverage of their speeches. The joke in the office was that they could screen the footage of the previous year's gala without the viewer noticing.

This troubled Sid. 'There must be a different way we can do this,' he was heard saying. The miners were his people, the gala was a joyous, boisterous event, surely they should do something that reflected that atmosphere? He worked closely with a director and kindred spirit named Ken Stephinson, and the pair were assigned to produce that year's package. They hit upon a wheeze: they would shoot the usual footage – marching, singing, playing, Harold Wilson waving – but they would cut it to 'Dancing In The Streets' by Martha and the Vandellas.

The package was screened, and everyone in the office thought it worked brilliantly. The viewer reaction was positive too. The idea of laying music over a news item was revolutionary: nothing like this had been done before. It was one thing to have two presenters walloping each other with newspapers aboard spacehoppers to some bouncy music, quite another to set one of the biggest news events of the year to a hit record.

Yet it nearly killed Sid and Ken's careers. While the public response had been overwhelmingly good, the Labour Party were unhappy. Harold Wilson's formidable press secretary Joe

Haines had erupted with fury when he saw pictures of Wilson apparently swaying to the music with a pipe in his mouth. Here were a bunch of cocky upstarts undermining his grand annual appearance by turning it into a promo for *Top of the Pops*. Wilson was not averse to gaining publicity by mixing with pop stars, notably the Beatles, but the gala was a chance to burnish his credentials as a man-of-the-people leader of the Labour movement, not an opportunity to chase the youth vote.

Haines called the powers that be at Tyne Tees demanding that those responsible for demeaning the office of prime minister and leader of the Labour Party be sacked. Rather than telling them to get stuffed, the complaint was taken with the utmost seriousness. Some in the boardroom had sympathy with Haines and believed Sid and Ken had turned news and current affairs into a circus, while even those who thought it brilliant television were aghast at upsetting the government of the day. Sid and Ken were doomed.

But in an act of solidarity and protest that would make a Labour leader proud, the other directors and producers at Tyne Tees threatened to quit if the pair were sacked. In the end, the management backed down, apologized to Haines and the Labour Party but stood by their men. Sid's career was saved, and with it the practice of overlaying music over a bland item of news: the musical montage was born.

Stalagmites and Stalactites

IN MY LAST year of primary school, we were to go away on a week-long trip. I could barely contain my excitement. For days before, I could speak of little else. About the only person I hadn't discussed it with was my dad. The evening before we left, he asked me about it. I told him we were going to Thorpe Hall in Fylingthorpe, North Yorkshire; that Philip Dibb had a digital watch you could play a game on, which he was bringing; and that on the way we were stopping off at Stump Cross Caverns.

'What's that?'

'Some caves, I think.'

'Great.'

'They have stalagmites and stalactites.'

Now I had his interest.

'Do you know the difference?

I gave it some thought. 'Er, not sure.'

'Do you want an easy way to remember?'

I nodded, eager for some fatherly wisdom.

'Down with the tites. Up with all your mite.'

I was ten years old.

But to be fair, I've never, ever forgotten the different between a stalactite and a stalagmite.

The Wild West of Leeds

I N JULY 1968, Yorkshire Television broadcast for the first time. Until then, despite being the country's biggest county, it had been bundled up with the North-West and served by Granada, based in Manchester, which caused endless grumbling over the right side of the Pennines. But now they had their own channel, and first on the list of its owners' priorities was to make a nightly news programme that reflected the spiky, diverse and eccentric nature of the county it served.

The result was *Calendar*, widely accepted in the industry to be the finest and most popular local news programme ever made. The man behind its creation was a Welshman named Donald Baverstock, who was often described as unpredictable, which in media terms is a euphemism for 'thirsty, talented and voluble'. As controller of programmes for BBC1, he had been instrumental in the creation of *Dr Who* in 1963. But his mercurial manner also created enemies, and in 1965 he resigned and joined the bid to win the Yorkshire Television franchise.

Once won, he became programme controller, and he started to handpick the men and women he wanted to produce *Calendar*. His selection criteria were based on his own whims and paid little heed to industry norms or even common sense. The first presenter he hired was Jonathan Aitken, future MP and jailbird, who was then prospective Tory MP for Thirsk and seeking a way to raise his profile in the North. As Aitken had gone to Eton and Christ Church, Oxford, and was a scion of the Beaverbrook family, Baverstock hired him even though he had no discernible talent for television whatsoever.

Other Baverstock recruits were no less eccentric but rather more successful. John Fairley was a suave, smooth-talking print journalist (and an Oxford graduate, naturally) but with no experience of television before joining YTV. Within a week of *Calendar*'s launch, he was programme editor. Bradford-born Austin Mitchell (Oxford) had spent most of the 1960s lecturing in sociology at a New Zealand university before returning to the UK. He joined YTV and swiftly became the face of *Calendar*, where the producers seemed to delight in making him run around after scantily clad women, a task he appeared willing to throw himself into.

Others arrived with more pedigree, among them two brusque, no-nonsense but experienced TV journalists: John Wilford and Barry Cockcroft. Presenter Liz Fox, who had worked with Sid at Tyne Tees, supplied both glamour and nous next to Aitken's inexperience, while a young Richard Whiteley slid on to a lower rung and bided his time until everyone grew tired of Aitken's awful stiltedness.

Sid arrived to add to this sprawl of characters in the summer of 1968. Soon to be a father-of-two, the extra money on offer was enough to lure him and Lindsey away from the North-East, and they settled in her hometown of York. His first day at the station's Kirkstall Road studios proved to be interesting. When he walked into the office, his former Granada colleague Cockcroft grabbed him by his lapels and pinned him against the wall.

'Some shitty things are going to happen today, and you better keep your mouth shut,' he growled.

Sid soon learned why: his former editor at Tyne Tees, Brian Gibson, hired to edit *Calendar*, was deposed in a studio putsch after a series of disastrous pilot programmes. He was replaced by the TV neophyte Fairley, while Sid wondered what the hell he had let himself in for.

This tumultuous beginning was to characterize his next six and a half years at YTV. This was television as the Wild West: a pioneering place of piss-ups, punch-ups and cock-ups, but where ideas flourished and reputations were made. Sid and other members of the *Calendar* crew became thick as thieves and pissed as farts; each day they went out and got stories and after the programme was screened they went out and got hammered. The next day, they rolled in with hangovers and did it all again. Thankfully, steady hands such as Scottish news editor Graham Ironside were able to ensure that a semblance of sanity reigned. No easy task, especially when the studio complex was finished and they opened the YTV bar, an act akin to giving Burke and Hare the keys to the mortuary. The fun was not confined to Kirkstall Road though; it spilled across Leeds and the dirty old town's pubs and restaurants: Whitelock's, 'the Scarbrough Taps', Get Stuffed, Jumbo Chinese restaurant, and the Flying Pizza in Roundhay. Unfortunately for my mother, at home with two, then three and finally four children with my arrival in 1972, Sid's reluctance to leave the conviviality of work for the domesticity of home had a predictable effect on their marriage.

In the rollicking culture at *Calendar*, Sid's eye for the offbeat and unorthodox was celebrated. When the likes of Barry Cockcroft uncovered arcane pastimes in the Yorkshire Dales like knell and spur, 'Yorkshireman's golf' as it was otherwise known, and milked it for all it was worth plus expenses, Sid saw it as a challenge to come up with an even better idea, though he resisted the temptation to revisit Dwile Flonking.

His career had started to flourish. Unlike Granada, where he never fitted in, or Tyne Tees, where his approach seemed at odds with the station's ethos, at YTV he had found a home of likeminded men and women, and a culture in which innovation and ideas were welcomed and not viewed with suspicion. Or, as he once put it to me: 'I was working with a bunch of loonies, and that suited my style.'

Not only was he a crucial part of *Calendar*'s success but his writing talents brought him other work and opportunities. Even though he went to Cambridge, which Donald Baverstock thought inferior to Oxford, the Welshman grew to love him. The feeling was mutual: Baverstock, Sid once said, 'was the epitome of creative vitality, with ideas bursting from him like a volcano'. However, sometimes the volcano erupted before the lava was ready to flow. Baverstock would journey down to London to meet fellow panjandrums at ITV, fortified by a few snifters en route, and boast about programmes he was making, which Lew Grade and other heads of ITV would be mad not to show across the entire network. The only problem was that these programmes didn't exist.

On one such occasion, he arrived back on a Friday afternoon

and rolled into the Queen, a spit and sawdust pub behind Yorkshire TV. Sid was in there, and Baverstock took him to one side.

'I've told Lew Grade that we're making an historical children's drama series about two boys,' he said.

'Are we?'

'We are now. I'll give you a hundred pounds if you come up with a script by Monday morning.'

It was a ludicrous task, but also more than three weeks' wages in one go. Sid went home, cloistered himself away and hit the typewriter. He drew upon his childhood love for Walter Scott and tales of derring-do, and a recent work visit to Harewood House on the outskirts of Leeds, and came up with the idea of *The Flaxton Boys* (Baverstock wanted to call it *The Boys of Nightingale Hall*, but, as Sid said to the website TV Heaven, it lacked 'consonantal bounce'), a drama featuring a decrepit stately home, mysterious characters, buried treasures and cryptic clues. Wild-eyed and sleep-deprived, he handed the opening episode to Baverstock first thing on Monday morning. Later that day, he was summoned back to his office. His boss loved it.

'Can I have the second episode by Wednesday?' he added.

The series had been Sid's creation, but ahead of its transmission on Sunday, 21 September 1969, he learned he was only to get a writing credit. This would mean fewer royalties should it be sold onwards. So, when the executive producer was away, he took out the woman responsible for compiling the closing credits, plied her with drink, and lo and behold there, as the credits rolled over the cresting, orchestral theme tune, were the words: 'Series originated by Sid Waddell'. The show was a critical and commercial success and ran for three series, though Sid's involvement shrank as other avenues opened up. But those drinks paid off: as originator, he still received small but welcome royalty cheques for years to come, including one from Taiwan.

Dreams of scriptwriting fame grew. He and John Wilford cloistered themselves away for two weeks, and fuelled by booze and adrenaline they wrote a comedy series called *Best of Order*, about a working men's club, a sort of proto *Phoenix Nights*. It attracted the interest of Les Dawson, a fixture in the YTV bar at the time, and Ken Dodd, who both agreed to take parts in it. It would have been the latter's first and only acting role. Sadly, no one was willing to put it into production; it languished in both men's desk drawers and is now lost to history. Wilford regrets that to this day: 'It was bloody good . . .' he says.

Advice

OCCASIONALLY, I WOULD find Sid in the back room of the house at 77 South Parade in Pudsey, sitting in a chair, hands clasped in front of his mouth, staring darkly. This meant someone or something had upset him. In these moments, he would occasionally mumble and talk to himself, as if working out an imaginary argument. If he had a drink inside him, there might even be bad language. 'Bastard . . . fucking bastard . . .'

He looked so troubled on this occasion that I asked him what was wrong. He was always someone you could approach, even in the darkest of moods. My words snapped him out of his reverie.

'What's that, kidda?'

'Is everything OK?'

'Yeah, fine, fine,' he said distractedly.

I nodded.

'Can I give you some advice?'

'Yes,' I said, only slightly apprehensive after his last bout of parental advice.

'Never, ever trust a man who doesn't drink.'

I was eleven years old.

Bedroll Bella

THE BOOK WAS slim, no more than 140 pages. Nothing about its sleek black cover with the photo of a seductive young woman in a denim hat and jacket suggested I shouldn't read it. After all, she was sucking on a red lollipop. I liked lollipops, though admittedly I hadn't seen anyone suck on them quite like *that*.

The blurb on the back hinted at something illicit.

Bedroll Bella . . . that was what they called her around the drop-out camps and Rock Festivals. A wild, black-haired hippy with good looks and a body to match. Bella walked out of her Tyneside home looking for freedom. She found it with Spider and his fellow drop-outs, easy-going, free-loving, thumbing their noses at disapproving society. Until Spider got hot for a new girl . . . and her Hell's Angel boyfriend put his boot in.

It sounded racy, but the first few pages were not. Bella is rebellious, cheeks off her mum and dad before attending her last day of grammar school, where she argues with her teacher about the workers and trade unions. So far, so dull. What the hell was a bedroll anyway?

Then one of Bella's mates gives a boy a hand job on the back of the bus.

Call me precious, but I'm not sure an eleven-year-old boy should read his father's graphic description of someone being wanked off. I put the book back and wondered if I should wash my hands.

Bedroll Bella was to be Sid's sideline, his ticket out of TV and into the world of novels, as well as some much-needed cash for him, his wife and four kids. It was published by Sphere in 1973, the same company that produced Timothy Lea's wildly success-ful *Confessions* series. Sid had written it to a similar template but changed the main character from a young man to a woman. It was a brave move: Sid, by his own admission later in life, was hardly reconstructed. He was the only man I knew outside a tabloid newsroom who used the word 'bonk', and employed the word 'knockers' as a synonym for breasts.

Both he and his publishers had hopes of success; Sid had even plotted out a series of further adventures for Bella. There was some publicity, including a piece in the *Yorkshire Post* where I made my first newspaper appearance as '11-month-old David'. On the day of publication, Sid had travelled to London, where he had ensconced himself in a pub to start a hefty session to toast the book's success.

After a few beers, and in the words of Sid, 'feeling no pain', his agent walked in, ashen-faced. Sid offered to buy him a drink, and he asked for a double Scotch.

'What's up, kidda?' Sid asked.

His agent sank the Scotch in one and asked for another.

'The publishers just phoned me,' he muttered.

'And?' Sid waited for some triumphant sales news. Perhaps a film adaption, just like the *Confessions* series.

'It's been banned.'

His agent went on to say that because of its explicitly sexual content, WHSmith and John Menzies had refused to sell it, effectively killing off any chance of success. According to Sid, bookshops and vendors had got frit as a result of Mary Whitehouse's Nationwide Festival of Light campaign, which sought to fight back against what she saw as the explicit depiction of sex and violence in the mass media. Selling a dirty novel with a cover featuring a young woman performing fellatio on a lollipop within range of impressionable young men and women was now frowned upon. Sid joined his agent on the heavy stuff, and his dreams of being a bestselling novelist were over.

That was how he told it anyway. The Festival of Light campaign had been launched in the early seventies but had run its course by 1973, when *Bella* was published. Neither were Smiths or Menzies known to withhold books for saucy content, and while *Bedroll Bella* is lewd and rude, it wasn't pornographic or corrupting (unless you were the pre-pubescent son of the author, who happened to chance upon the paragraph where a young woman is given the nickname 'Gobble 'n' Chuff' because 'certain privileged parties at the school had been treated to her offering of a suck-off while you tickled her bum'.)

It makes a far less compelling story, but it's more likely that the two bookshops chose not to stock it because their buyers didn't think it was very good. The simple truth is that it isn't. It's very much of its time, and so hard to judge by today's standards, but the plot is as skimpy as Bella's much-described knickers. She leaves her Tyneside home behind, goes to work at a holiday camp, runs off with a bunch of counterculture types, finds enlightenment and then disillusionment and crawls home to Geordieland. In the meantime, Bella's frequent erotic experiences leave her unsatisfied, much like the reader.

However, there is plenty of evidence of my dad's ability to turn a colourful and arresting phrase: 'The pavement was washed in the saffron-sodium light of streetlamps' . . . 'Then sex reared its ugly head and the gilt washed off the gingerbread' . . . 'When the sun comes out hot and strong, the popular south side of Scarborough is like a giant chip pan. It bubbles with life – hot, sweaty northern life – and it smells: of seaweed, hot dogs, chips, people, but mainly hot dogs' . . . 'The air of Tyneside is the gruel of life; its pubs are the meaty morsels that give the whole thing flavour.'

Sentences like this belong in a different book, and it's a much better one. Given a different subject and genre, it might have been a different story. I think Sid knew it too; the story doesn't end in cliché, with the heroine in the arms of her hometown sweetheart, or in the embrace of her simple but loving mum and dad, but with Bella finishing the final words of a sonnet she has been contemplating: 'The firefly glows on summer haze / But melts to ash in winter's blaze.' All in all, it seems a shame he wasted his *Bildungsroman* by ladling on a ton of badly written smut.

There is also a strong, revealing autobiographical element. Bella is clever and erudite, and this otherness has alienated her from her working-class mum and dad; she spends her time, as Sid did, dreaming of bigger and better and wilder; she likes rock 'n' roll and literature and poetry, as well as raucous pubs and the larger-than-life characters that populate them. In a passage that could have come straight from Sid's memoirs, she even shares his Catholic guilt:

> Her mam came of Irish labouring people and had dragged Bella out of bed for Mass, Communion and all the jazz on a thousand cold Sunday mornings. Now Bella was totally and utterly lapsed as far as the Faith was concerned. Her mother could say a million Hail Marys and umpteen Apostle's creeds – but no penance would get Bella back to the Holy Water show.

Whatever its flaws, Sid was proud of *Bedroll Bella* for three reasons. The first was obvious: it was a published novel, an ambition realized, albeit briefly. Few achieve that. Second, its ban for explicit sexual content, whether true or not, gave him a great story, which he told countless times to willing reporters and feature writers, who in turn lapped it up.

Finally, but perhaps most significantly, he believed he was the first fiction writer to employ the phrase 'vinegar stroke' (the last thrust by a man during sex before ejaculation, coined because the expression on his face resembles that of one drinking neat vinegar). There is no reason to dispute this.

I also doubt Jean Rhys or Angela Carter employed the phrase 'gravy feeling' to describe the female orgasm.

Any Port in a Storm

I DON'T KNOW WHO they were, but we had friends over. This was a rare occurrence. Irene and Sid did socialize, in their respective work bars mainly, but not often at home. The weekends were a chance to rest and read and recharge for both of them. But this evening, there were guests and they were downstairs.

The problem was that no one could find Sid.

He had called in from Leeds station, so he had made it back. Irene said he sounded like he'd had a few, but that was not uncommon. But how many was a few?

Search parties were sent to the local pubs to see if he had dropped in on his way home, but he couldn't be found. It reached the stage where people were getting worried. Had there been an accident? Had he been mugged? Was he lying helpless and stricken in a gutter? Irene started to consider phoning around the hospitals.

It was my sister Emma who found him, following the sound of soft snores. He was in the walk-in cupboard in his and Irene's bedroom, asleep on a pile of clothes on the floor. The smell of booze was pungent and sweet.

'I've found him,' she shouted.

The Indoor League

Rooting through the scraps of paper and folders of cuttings and old programmes and notes in Sid's archive, I came across a thin book, less than a hundred pages long. It was a book that accompanied *The Indoor League*, the series about pub sports he created in 1972. I never knew it existed or heard him mention it. Clearly, it was thrown together to make a quick buck on the back of the programme's surprise success. It was written together with his fellow producer John Meade, but as I read the prologue, its voice was pure Sid.

We live in an age whose technology can not only allow 250 million people to see men walk live on the moon, but can also let seven million in on the intimate secrets of the shove ha'penny ace. We are proud to be part of that second TV breakthrough. And we would suggest it is the bigger achievement. All of us, from lovers to shovers, have been able to *see* the moon over the years; but until the *Indoor League* cameras broke apart the huddle, shove ha'penny was confined to a live audience of six or seven fanatics crouched over a bit of shiny teak.

I'd go as far as saying that opening paragraph could not have been written by anyone else, ever. It features so many of those verbal props and tricks that characterized his television commentaries that it could act as his philosophy, his *Weltanschauung*, his manifesto. There is the bathos of comparing the moon landing to a game of shove ha'penny; the hyperbole in believing televising the latter was a greater achievement; and the dexterous wordplay that rhymes lovers and shovers. All delivered with tongue firmly in cheek but also with the utmost sincerity. He believed these men were capable of great feats, and he believed that bringing those feats to the screen was an important step for ordinary men and women, hitherto ignored or patronized by television.

His love of darts and darts players was real and would grow, but the pastime he admired most was shove ha'penny. He played himself, rather better than he did darts, and once claimed to be shove ha'penny champion of Yorkshire, only later admitting he claimed this crown by beating Fred Trueman in a one-off game in a pub on the outskirts of York. It simply turned out that of all the events covered by *The Indoor League*, darts was the most televisual. It would lend itself perfectly to the format, whereas the nuances and deftness of shove ha'penny, despite his grandiose claims, did not reveal themselves on TV, nor could it match the posturing drama that made darts such a success.

The book has a section devoted to each pub game featured in *The Indoor League*: arm-wrestling, table football, shove ha'penny, men's and ladies' darts, cheese skittles, table skittles, bar billiards and American pool. Each chapter is introduced by italicized prose extolling either the game's virtues or those of its finest competitors. So table footballer Speedy Campbell, the

'Johan Cruyff of the plastic striker', has 'hair like a black Brillo pad, eyes like best nutty slack and wrists as supple as Damascus steel', while Welsh darts legend Alan Evans, a man whom Sid would take to his very heart, was described as 'the Cochise of the concentric rings'. There is also a potted history of each game, given a Sid spin: arm-wrestling had been around 'since Cain slew Abel' apparently, whereas Henry VIII 'between wife-napping and wife-swapping' popularized table skittles, and Dr Johnson 'so Boswell tells us, was a mean hand on the set down at the local coffee shop'.

But the blood and guts of the book is the opening of the section on shove ha'penny, which since publication, and the book sold only a few hundred copies then, has remained 'blushing unseen', as the poet once said. It begins with the description of a full Durham pub on a Saturday night. In the smoke and the throng, Big Mitch and Melvin are embroiled in a match that has those present entranced.

The two-foot-six of teak playing area gleamed like Roker Park floodlit and needing a dollop or two of sand. Mitch sniffed and fingered the dab of French chalk, used to score because it leaves no grease on the board. His fingers cranked the five coins, his arm flexed like Nureyev working up a sweat at the limbering bar. Gently the coins eased in the three inches below the base line; Mitch's stubby fingers worked them like a knock-kneed spider, urging them to get a feel of the board . . . Shove ha'penny demands more concentration than darts, but the touch must be as light as a butterfly's eyelash. Mitch was built like a Nubian midwife.

The match builds to its climax. Melvin wins with an audacious shot that rests triumphantly in bed two.

'Game shot,' whistled Tommy behind the bar. Mitch sniffed, sneered, downed his ale, tightened his muffler a couple of notches.

'I'm off to the Vic,' he announced.

'Don't have a rum and black then,' said Melvin for effect. Their eyes would have cut steel-plate. Mitch left.

'Lend me two quid and fill the bar,' said Melvin quietly.

Thus the drama, the tragedy and the triumph of matchplay nudging amongst the Durham mafia.

∽

There is a belief among some that *The Indoor League* was where TV darts was born. This is somewhat unfair to the visionaries at ITV sport, who decided to televise the first *News of the World* final from Alexandra Palace for *World of Sport*. Dave Lanning, a journalist with the *TV Times* by day but whose speedway commentaries were already a thrilling mainstay of the programme, was chosen to commentate, and he could not believe the sight that met him in Muswell Hill: twelve thousand fans creating a wave of noise that exceeded even the most fervent football game. The players, who had won through heats and round in pubs and bars all over the country to attend the finals, walked out to a colossal, guttural roar. The star was a short, chubby Welshman named Alan Evans, who made up in charisma what he lacked in stature.

When Dave left, wading ankle-deep through beer and piss,

to return to LWT's studios for the post-programme beer and sandwiches, he soon realized they had struck a nerve. The phones were red-hot with those calling to praise the coverage and demand more, while head of sport John Bromley handed out hero-grams. No one could quite believe how well it had worked on television. The director that day was another Welshman, Peter Jones, seconded from Yorkshire Television.

He raced back to Leeds and babbled enthusiastically about what he had seen. Sid was entranced, and he had an idea. They went to Donald Baverstock's office, and through a cloud of cigar smoke Jones recounted his experiences, and Sid waxed poetic about the nimble nudgers of the Durham shove ha'penny tables. Baverstock did not need much convincing, having witnessed the virtuosity of table skittlers during his South Wales upbringing. And so the potpourri of pastimes that formed *The Indoor League* was born.

Sid's first task as producer was to line up as many competitors as possible. This involved him and a team of researchers fanning out across the pubs of the North to find the best darters, shovers and skittlers. The more colourful and outlandish the better, hence characters such as Buffalo Bill, a shover who dressed in full cowboy regalia complete with holster and a cap gun.

On Peter Jones' recommendation, Sid hired Dave Lanning to commentate on the darts, so beginning an intermittent working relationship, and an enduring friendship that lasted for the next forty years. Dave remembers being met by Sid from the train at Leeds, starting the day with a pint at the Queens Hotel and ending it with the pair of them in the Jumbo Chinese restaurant, high on life and lager, singing, 'They tried to sell us egg foo yung' to a group of bewildered Cantonese waiters and punters.

Next on the list was a presenter. As it had a quintessential Northern flavour, he picked a quintessential Northern man: Yorkshire and England fast-bowling legend Fred Trueman, famous for saying what he liked and liking what he bloody well said. He had recently gone into stand-up comedy, but that did not translate into ease in front of the camera. His links during that first series have all the fluidity of a treacle sponge, but he improved, and his cardigans, wide-lapelled shirts, but most of all his greeting 'Nah then' and sign-off 'Aye'll sithee', with a sloshing pint of bitter in hand, are what most people remember.

The heats were held nightly in the Yorkshire TV studios and screened on *Calendar*, with the finals held in a function room at the Queens Hotel beside Leeds station, a place where Sid had supped many a pint before and after a train journey. Filming took place over two days in October 1972, and it's fair to say Sid was nervous over how it would turn out. The task of capturing the action of a simultaneous array of pub games, while providing the contestants with unlimited free booze, was both ambitious and foolhardy. By his own admission, they shot everything that moved and hoped for the best. The edit would take weeks. But by the end they had a programme that illuminated a sporting subculture and was impressive enough to encourage the bosses at ITV to order a second series for a national audience.

That first series is more than dated: there are baby mammoths plucked from the Arctic ice and thawed out that have aged better. The camera angle on the darts means Dave Lanning can't see if shots have been made, while the decision to play it on a Yorkshire board minus trebles means the featured matches are interminable, though the darts feels mercifully brief compared to the nine-minute game of table football in which poor Keith Macklin, normally a rugby league commentator, tries vainly to find a vocabulary to fit four students from Leeds Uni twiddling knobs, the ball a blur when it isn't being jettisoned from the table. Meanwhile, Fred lurches on and off screen with his pint and pipe, delivering some menacing links. 'Sithee in a tick,' he says before the commercial break, more as a warning than an invite. Apparently, he had moaned when he first saw Sid's script.

'I don't talk like this,' he said.

'You do now,' he was told by executive producer John Fairley.

Yet the whole thing works and charms, not least because of the way the programme revels in the characters and competitors and never seeks to look down on them. Sid also plucks out a story or two to weave through the series, so by the end the viewer thinks they know those involved.

By the second series, screened nationally, the production team didn't have to go out and find players; the players came to them. One morning Sid was called by Olly Croft of the Greater London Darts Organisation, who told him the players he had on the first series were crap and that he could provide him with better ones. Impressed by his cheek and audacity, Sid took up his offer, and the show improved because of it. The Welsh contingent also turned up, including Sid's favourite, Alan Evans. Unlike the lads in the first series, who played in suit and tie or cardigans, the new, brasher lot wore loud shirts with their names emblazoned across the back and swigged beer before, during and after their matches. *The Indoor League* book revealed that Evans' 'drinking number was eight', referring to how many pints he needed to attain his ideal state for darts.

The Leeds Irish Centre was chosen as the show's new venue and would be for subsequent series. Its atmosphere made the Queens Hotel look like a parlour party. It grew increasingly rowdy, to the extent that filming for the third series was curtailed by a riot. It kicked off at the table football when one player celebrated a goal by punching the air but connected with his opponent. Tanked up on free ale, others piled in, and the saloon brawl soon grew into a cartoon mass punch-up, with balls of people and arms and legs flying, and pots of beer and tables and chairs soaring through the air. When everyone had cleared out, the damage was negligible bar some broken glass and furniture, but after losing half a day's filming they needed somewhere the next day to complete the rest.

Sid targeted the Belle Isle Working Men's Club in Beeston and launched a charm offensive that started on the phone to the secretary and ended with him offering an impassioned plea for help to the committee at an emergency meeting that evening. They were persuaded, and the series was salvaged.

Fred's links became ever more outrageous as Sid and his team relaxed into their roles. Handsome arm-wrestler Mark Sinclair-Scott was also a male model, so Sid labelled him the 'Narcissus of the knotted knuckles', though Fred in his first take mangled it so it became 'the nancy boy with the knotted knuckles'. Other scripted moments of genius included a reference to a crack shove ha'penny player as the 'Spassky of the sliding small change', while Trueman promised 'The Kings of Darts will steal your heart.'

~

Sid would produce another series in 1974 before his abrupt departure from YTV. But the show would continue under the eye of his amanuensis, John Meade. JB as he was universally known – or 'Gay B' innocently by one of my sisters – was as thirsty as any darts player, and his private life was a saga. After being kicked out of the flat he rented when the landlord, a noted freelance TV producer, saw the state it was in, he stored his belongings in the cellar of our house in Pudsey. Along with his rowing machine and golf clubs was his entire collection of pornographic books and magazines, which made *Bedroll Bella* look like the *Beano*, and which my sisters and I would browse with some wonder. Irene never knew about them until a builder who was doing some work on the house told her about them, and they swiftly disappeared. Despite his chaotic nature, JB did a good job with *The Indoor League* after Sid's departure until its demise in 1978 and would go on to produce the rather more sober and sedate *Countdown* for Channel Four.

World of Sport and the *News of the World* might have beaten Sid to the claim to have been the first to screen modern darts, but *The Indoor League* can claim to be the spiritual birth of darts as we now know it. It revelled in the darters' larger-than-life characters and the culture that bred them. In its pomp, it attracted seven million viewers, and Sid was proud to have made television stars out of coal miners, steel workers and, 'let's be blunt, some lads who neither work nor want'.

Everybody Out!

WE WERE ALL upstairs in bed apart from Irene, who was decorating the back room. She had been painting every night after work for more than a week. It was a backbreaking job, because the new house we'd moved into in 1983 was big, and the rooms had high ceilings and cornices. But all the money had gone on buying the place and making it habitable – the previous owners had lived there for decades without central heating and with flock wallpaper and two strip lights dangling from the ceiling of the sitting room like a post-war operating theatre.

Irene knew she couldn't count on Sid to help. For a start, DIY wasn't his thing. He never changed so much as a plug. Not because he was lazy but because he didn't have any basic competence. There would be a risk of a lot of swearing and the house becoming engulfed in an electrical fire. I never saw him mend or fix anything. Or cook anything, though I did show him how to make a basic bolognese, involving onions, mince and some pasta sauce. I came back from uni once and he told me how he had cooked it himself, as proud as he was about one of his books. He could also boil an egg. That was the extent of his repertoire though.

He had his chores. Washing up was one, always performed with a tea towel over his shoulder. After Sunday lunch, while Irene the chef relaxed with a Rothmans and the Sunday newspapers, Sid would start to wash the pots. 'I need a team,' he said every week, which meant the rest of us. Our job was to dry and put away, or put to one side his shoddy washing work for another quick rinse later. When Irene bought a dishwasher, Sid was crestfallen. One of his main reasons for domestic existence had been cruelly snatched from him and handed to a machine. 'I can see now why there's nae work for any bugger any more,' he told me forlornly, eyeing the dishwasher with some aggression. Out of protest he refused to learn how to stack and use it properly, and occasionally, illicitly and furtively, washed dishes by hand.

As compensation, he found the washing machine. Irene taught him how to programme it, to add the soap and fabric softener. He'd head down to the cellar with a basket of washing – pre-sorted into colours – a tea towel defiantly draped over his shoulder, and set it going. Then when it was done, with a floral peg-bag around his neck, he'd hang it out on the line.

Religiously, every Saturday morning he would perform another chore. He'd go through the cupboards and the fridge to do a stocktake for that week's shop. On a piece of paper, he would dutifully draw two columns, 'Got' and 'Need', and make notes: 'Got' two eggs; 'Need' four eggs. And so on. Then he and Irene would shop, coming home with the back of their Peugeot Estate crammed with bags. Sid would burst through the door with a shout of 'Every-body out!' and me, my sisters and stepbrother Nick would be expected to unload the car and then put away the shopping. Even when I was the last person left at home, he would open the door after a trip to the supermarket and say 'Every-body out!' According to Irene, he did it after I left and there was no one in to be out. My sister Charlotte admits that even when she gets back from Waitrose and opens the door with hands full of shopping she can't resist shouting 'Every-body out', to the frequent bewilderment of her kids.

His lack of practical aptitude did mean there was money to be made for an enterprising child. He was quite particular about the length he wanted his trousers and often paid Charlotte to take them up or let them down. One time he gave her a pair of slacks and indicated with thumb and index finger how much he wanted them taken up by. 'Just that much,' he emphasized. Charlotte put them on the back of a chair to attend to later.

Two days later, my dad walked in wearing the slacks. 'You've done a grand job with these, our lass,' he said, giving a twirl. 'Absolutely spot on,' and he handed her a crisp five-pound note. 'Good work.'

Charlotte hadn't touched the trousers. She'd forgotten all about them, but Sid had been in, tried them on and liked what he thought he saw.

She pocketed the cash. Just as I did one day when he asked me to trim the hedge and I forgot. But he came back and congratulated me on some decent graft and handed over another fiver.

The garden was his domain. Which isn't to say he was a gardener. He planted nothing, knew the name of no plants and did no watering or weeding. By now there was a gardener who did that, and Irene if he was unavailable. But Sid and no one else raked the leaves and mowed the lawn. The latter he viewed as exercise, a release. I was a journalist working at an agency in

York when Princess Diana died. There was so little room in the papers for any other news that we had been given a few days off. On the day of her funeral, I was back in Pudsey, and even though we were hardly ardent royalists, Irene and I sat down together to watch the funeral. Sid was having none of it.

'Ah'm off to mow the lawn,' he said when Elton John popped up.

'No, you're not, Sid,' said Irene.

'Why not?'

I could see Irene trying to find the right words without sounding like a suck-up to the royals.

'The neighbours will be watching the funeral, and the sound of the mower will distract them. It'll be like making a noise during a minute's silence.'

'Bollocks,' he said. 'I'm not sitting here and watching this shite.' And off he went to mow the lawn while we watched the final act of England's collective loss of sense.

～

Back when we'd moved in, one night he did do an hour or two with the roller on the wall, leaving Irene to do the difficult bits while he slept. Until there was a massive crash and a scream. It was definitely Irene. I sat bolt upright in my bed as my dad crashed out of his bedroom, thankfully still wearing a pair of pants below his T-shirt. But instead of heading downstairs, he went next door into Charlotte and Emma's bedroom.

'Quick,' he said. 'One of you go downstairs and see if Rene's all right. I think she's fallen off the stepladder.'

Bravery might not have been one of his strong points either.

Revie and Rupture

ALONGSIDE *THE INDOOR LEAGUE*, Sid was given freedom at YTV to work on other documentaries. One was about the Charlton brothers, Bobby and Jackie, written by Arthur Hopcraft, whose book *The Football Man* remains one of the finest accounts ever written of the sport. As the Charltons had been born and raised in Ashington, a mile or so away from Sid, it offered a chance to revisit his roots.

His next project involved an even spikier football figure: Don Revie, the Leeds United manager. The 1973–74 season was to be the last of Revie's successful tenure, crowned with their second league title, before he replaced Sir Alf Ramsey as England manager. Sid was charged with making a documentary about Revie's career at Leeds, entitled *The Don of Elland Road*.

The result was an extraordinary, intimate portrait of an often impenetrable, enigmatic character. Sid gained access to his office, the training ground, fitness tests that Revie held in public parks, the dugout, the game of pre-match bingo, the team coach and the dressing room. He even filmed Revie helping to rub down and massage his naked players after training, which, it's fair to say, Brian Clough didn't do when he famously and briefly succeeded him at the end of that season. At one stage he is filmed lounging on a pink floral bedspread, reading the newspapers and speaking on the phone before his wife brings him breakfast on a tray the day after Leeds had lost at Anfield to title rivals Liverpool.

'How did you sleep? All right?' she asks.

'Not so well,' he says. 'Played the match all over again . . .'

The film culminates in a thumping 4–1 loss at home to Burnley, the home side's first defeat at Elland Road for two years, and Revie's candid philosophizing over his evening meal, which is sitting on the same silver tray we saw earlier. 'It spoils your steak, you don't enjoy your weekend . . . it takes you until Monday morning to get over it. But when I see the lads' faces, I can lift myself.' They went on to win the title by five points.

Revie has never been shown as unguarded before or since. It's a remarkable film, by far the best Sid ever produced. And how he managed to convince such a cautious man to open up and allow him and his crew such unfettered access – to the point where we see Revie's hands vigorously rubbing Paul Reaney's soaped-up arse – is testament to Sid's power of charm and persuasion.

It came at a cost though, both literally and metaphorically. Revie was notorious for liking money. Meanwhile, YTV were not in the habit of paying for programmes. To get round this, Sid was transporting carrier bags of cash in secret to hand to Revie as payment for his cooperation. He was then reclaiming this money by fiddling his expenses. This was common practice in journalism and part of the warp and weft of YTV, where Barry Cockcroft among others turned it into a fine art. But such was the quantity of cash he was handing to Revie, Sid needed his expenses on time to avoid plunging him and our family into debt we could ill afford. If John Fairley, who signed off expenses, wasn't around on a Friday, Sid couldn't afford to not have his cash. So he took to forging his signature.

It's not clear how many times he did it. But late in 1974, after the Revie programme had been screened, he did it once more for reasons unknown. This time it was spotted, and when someone went back through previous claims, his forgeries were uncovered. Paul Fox, who had replaced Donald Baverstock as programme director, sacked him on the spot. John Fairley remembers going for lunch in Leeds with Sid in the office, but by the time he returned, Sid's desk had been cleared.

The stress on my mother and father's relationship had been growing for some time. His sacking did not help and placed the family under enormous financial strain. Sid had little time to mope about; he needed to find a job. The good news was that he found one starting in the New Year; the bad news was that it was in Iran.

~

How he got the job in Tehran working for National Iran Radio and Television (NIRT) is unclear, but it seems likely he answered an advertisement in *Broadcast*. This was four years before the Islamic Revolution and the fall of the Shah, and with a growing budget NIRT was seeking to hire experienced foreign producers, directors and cameramen.

In that regard, Sid fitted the bill. In many others, he didn't. He was not an experienced foreign traveller, and he was terrified of flying; until late in life he needed to fortify himself with alcohol to muster the courage to board a plane. He took the job thinking he was going to establish the newsroom in Tehran along the lines of *Calendar*. To his horror, he was instructed to work as assistant producer on a programme named *Special Correspondent*, visiting different cities across the world for a hectic few weeks of filming, trying to boil down the chosen place's culture and politics into one hour of television. Each week he needed to fly Iran Air to places such as Bangkok, Tokyo and Greece to make a documentary.

His boss was the fearless Javad Alamir-Davaloo, foreign commentator of NIRT but also *Le Monde*'s correspondent in Iran. As well as the programme, he edited a controversial magazine named *This Week in Tehran*. Religious groups tried to assassinate him in a bomb blast but only succeeded in injuring one of the magazine's staff. Like many others, Alamir-Davaloo fled Tehran in 1979 before the Islamic Revolution, an act that almost certainly saved his life.

Thankfully, Sid was not there to witness any of that. The insane schedule, the travel, the endless flying, the crazy Australian cameramen and the strange atmosphere all conspired to make him uneasy. Within three months he came back, unpaid and so skint that he needed to borrow the money for his train fare north from Dave Lanning.

On his return to Leeds, his and Lindsey's marriage ended. The previous two years had been tumultuous, with separations and reconciliations. But in May 1975 it was over for good.

In the aftermath, Sid took me, Charlotte, Emma and Lucy to Lynemouth, where we spent two weeks, and this might explain why it became such a haven for me as I grew up. There, in contrast to home, it was peaceful and calm.

But crowded. Unbeknown to Sid, my auntie Iris had left Derrick, stationed in Germany, and gone with Robbie to my grandparents', to whom she was very close. When we arrived, poor Martha and Bob were faced with the disintegration of two marriages and seven traumatized people to house in a two-bedroom cottage with no bath and an outside toilet. They didn't bat an eyelid, but I think Martha kept a steady pour on the gin.

I was too young to take in what was happening and have no conscious memory of that time, but for my sisters Charlotte, Emma and Lucy, five, seven and nine respectively, it was traumatizing. Life had not been sweetness and light, but one moment we lived in a nice house in Roundhay, the next we were squeezed into a two-up two-down miles away from home.

After two weeks, we returned to Roundhay, with Iris and Robbie. The idea was that Sid would search for work, while Iris looked after us until my mum was in a position to house us. It meant a semblance of normality for my sisters, and they could return to school. But it soon became clear that the house needed to be sold for financial reasons. Sid had no work, and the only way to raise cash for him and Lindsey was to sell the house.

When Sid and Lindsey had separated before, he became involved with Irene Cockroft, a researcher at Yorkshire Television who had worked her way up from the secretarial pool. But their relationship ended when Sid and Lindsey got back together. By now it was August, the house was about to be sold, Sid couldn't afford to rent anywhere, and the girls needed a school. Irene offered her end-of-terrace, three-bedroomed house in Pudsey as a temporary home until we went to live with my mum.

All this was a shock for her son Nick, whose peaceful life as an only child was abruptly interrupted by the arrival of four gobby kids and their gobby dad, as well as Iris, still estranged from Derrick, and her son Robbie. The house in Pudsey was an upgrade on Lynemouth: the toilet was indoors and there was one more bedroom. Sid renewed his hunt for a job, my three sisters enrolled at a primary school that was literally a stone's throw away, and Iris got a job at the Golden Lion until she and Derrick got back together. ('The best barmaid I ever had,' the landlord would say through misty eyes for several months afterwards.) I bunked up with Nick, the girls shared the two other rooms, while Sid and Irene slept on a put-up bed downstairs.

Unsurprisingly, given the upheaval, I became a needy child. When people left the house, I'd cling to their leg, begging them not to go, even if they were only going to the shop. I vaguely remember hanging on to a crying Sid for an age in South Parade when he left to go filming, and in my recollection he was more upset than I was. But it might explain why even now I can't stomach goodbyes. For a long time I couldn't enjoy a party because I knew it had to end.

My sisters were more affected. Having watched their parents' marriage break up acrimoniously, and been forced to leave their friends and school and their house behind, they found themselves in a new town, without friends and forced to start anew. For Charlotte and even Emma, this was easier to do as they were less settled and established in their old school. But for Lucy it was desperately hard. These were difficult times for all of us, not least for Nick, whose life had been invaded, and rows and tears and upset were common. Occasionally, Sid's lachrymosity, self-pity and fondness for seeking liquid solace didn't help, while Irene had an increasingly successful career she was not going to endanger for four kids who would not be there permanently, no matter how charming they might be. But through it all, my sisters and I remained close and we still are: adversity forges an unbreakable bond.

My mother visited us frequently, and I think it was everyone's belief that we would soon go and live with her. But a few weeks became a few months, my sisters settled in their school, made friends, and Irene and Sid made plans to extend the house to accommodate us all. Soon it became clear that to uproot us once more might cause further damage, and Lindsey and Sid decided that it might be preferable if we stayed put. Pudsey became our home. We would move to a more spacious house on the same street, where Irene and Sid would live until a few months before he died. No one would have known looking at us then, transient kids and an out-of-work dad, that Pudsey would become our home and the house we shared would become a haven we always returned to, where the wine and talk and stories flowed deep into the night.

Club Xenon

Perhaps reflecting the man at its head, we were an unconventional and often dysfunctional family. There were rows, and there was noise and trouble. My sister Charlotte became particularly rebellious: she was caught shoplifting at Asda, climbed over the roof of our primary school and watched as her friend smeared dogshit on the socks of a local vicar's daughter. This met with a rather ungodly reaction from the girl's father, who poured a kettle of cold water over Charlotte's head and not her guilty friend's. She thought it was boiling and ran home screaming. Once she realized she had not been burned and calmed down, Irene discovered what had happened. She strode round to the vicar's house, where he was left in no doubt that he had shamed his profession and his Boss upstairs. Neither was anyone in the streets surrounding. 'Call yourself a man of the cloth?!' was probably the most printable phrase I can recall.

Emma retreated into books and music and daydreams. She mastered the art of reading while rocking and sucking her thumb at the same time, and did it so often that her feet wore out the carpet where they slid back and forth as she rocked and read. Lucy escaped into being a teenager, with her friends and her boyfriends with their New Romantic hairdos and puffy shirts, while Nick just tried to keep his head down and out of our way. Meanwhile, I cried and threw what Sid called 'wobblers', not least when the 1978 World Cup final was on and I was the only one in the room supporting Argentina and was teased by the others when Holland scored first. No one told me it was a military junta. Likewise, when we were promised that we would go rambling in the Dales and I had a meltdown when it turned out to be a long walk. 'This isn't rambling,' I wailed. 'This is just walking around.'

Sid was still quoting that when I was forty.

Thankfully, Nick and Lucy soon got their own rooms, as did I, while Irene and Sid finally moved off the downstairs sofa and we all had a bit of space to spread out. Gradually, out of the pandemonium a sort of *esprit de corps* emerged, which manifested itself in a series of chaotic and eventful family holidays. The neighbours would look on with consternation as we set off, all seven of us crammed into a Volkswagen Beetle, children and belongings hanging out of the windows. Where Sid did excel, where he always excelled, was in leading a sing-song to while away interminable journeys with a car full of fractious kids and teenagers. He started off with a long version of 'On Top Of Old Smokey', with a few improvised verses of his own thrown in. This would then segue into 'Three Wheels On My Wagon' and continue from there.

We would join in between mouthfuls of Opal Fruits (incidentally the only sweet Sid knew – and about which he crowbarred a joke into his later television show, *Jossy's Giants*. The girl was Opal, she kissed Harvey and then tweaked his nose. 'Opal's cute,' said his mate. 'Yeah, made to make your eyes water,' said Harvey). Meanwhile, Irene drove endlessly with only Rothmans and service-station coffee to sustain her.

The first trip was to France, where Sid's disastrous map-reading skills caused us to become embedded on the plinth of a statue in Boulogne in the dead of night. We arrived after what felt like a week of travel, and Sid managed to persuade some YTV friends we met there to put up our tent while he and Irene drank wine. Just as well: Sid couldn't change a bedsheet, never mind put up a tent. Then Charlotte, Lucy and I came down with chickenpox. Mine were in my mouth, which made me even more whiny than usual. The long drive home was so traumatic it has been erased from all our memories.

As a result, the next few holidays were confined to the UK. By the time of Anglesey, thanks to Nick, I had developed a love of cricket. What I didn't love was being out. I would rope Nick and my sisters into a family game, but really all I wanted was for them to field and bowl at me. The first afternoon in Wales, I was at the crease when I was bowled. I disagreed with the decision, and when it was pointed out my stumps had been uprooted, I picked one of them up and threw it over the fence like a javelin, where it missed the head of the next-door neighbour by inches.

Lucy took me round when I had calmed down, and I apologized, which the elderly gentleman accepted graciously. Later that day, Sid took a stroll to the pub at the end of the road. The neighbour was sitting outside nursing a pint. His eyes narrowed as Sid approached.

'Are you Daniel's dad?'

'Aye,' said Sid.

'Are you moving in?'

'No. We're here on holiday.'

Relief swept across the man's face. 'Let me buy you a drink.'

I grew out of such tantrums once I realized that Sid and my sisters mocked me mercilessly the angrier I got, though it probably helped that they soon lost interest in playing cricket with a tyrannical kid. Nick was by now old enough to do his own thing, which he gladly did, while we headed abroad. By now, all my sisters were teenagers and presented a different kind of problem. Sid and I had sport and darts to share, but his relationship with my sisters was different. Charlotte was equally sporty for a time, and Sid once memorably enlivened a school netball match of hers by shouting 'Kill! Kill! Kill!' from the sidelines.

But it's fair to say that teenage girls were a mystery to him, as he discovered when we went to Pesaro in Italy in 1983. First of all, none of my sisters wanted to share a room with me. They would not even be bribed into it. So the only solution was for me to sleep on the spare bed in Irene and Sid's room, which ruined the romantic vibe they were hoping to establish.

While Irene and the girls got ready for dinner, Sid would take me on a trawl of a local bar or two for a beer and a Coke. Neither Irene nor Sid earned enough at that time to keep us in luxury, so every penny had to be spent wisely. 'Sip it,' Sid would say, planting my bottle of pop on the table and wagging a finger. He got into such a habit of this that he said it to me when he started buying me harder drinks as a man. 'Sip it,' he'd say, handing me a pint of lager, still wagging his finger.

So he was delighted when we found a bar where the handsome young waiter said the drinks were on the house. The next night it was the same. But I could see Sid starting to worry:

perhaps he would be presented with an enormous bill that he wouldn't be able to afford and then be beaten up by some Italian heavies. The next evening, when the waiter brought our complimentary drinks, Sid summoned the courage to ask why the drinks were free. A huge grin spread across the man's face.

'Signore,' he said. 'You have three very beautiful daughters.'

With me out from under their feet, it turned out that Lucy, Emma and Charlotte were feigning going to bed but instead sneaking out late and heading for Club Xenon, located beneath the hotel, where our waiter and his friends were regular patrons.

Sid looked at me and shrugged. 'Fair enough. We'll have another beer and a Coke then, kidda.'

Back at the hotel, the issue was thrashed out. My sisters apologized and were allowed to continue clubbing as long as they obeyed reasonable curfews. One thing bugged Sid though: how did the waiter know he was their father?

The girls supplied the answer. Sid in his tight red shorts, ice-white socks, oversized shades and man bag on his shoulder had become a minor celebrity in Pesaro.

'Who's the gay guy?' one Italian boy asked my sisters as they watched him walk around the pool.

'Our dad.'

The Prince of Dartness

B Y THE SUMMER of 1975, Sid's life, previously in chaos, assumed some normality. We had a new family home in Pudsey; he had a new partner and a determination to rebuild his television career, starting with a dip into something he knew well – darts. He travelled over the Pennines for a meeting with Ray Colley, the much-respected head of news and features at BBC North West in Manchester, and persuaded him to let him film darts' most charismatic character, Alan Evans, then based in Stockport.

Ever since he clapped eyes on 'Rhondda Fats' Alan Evans on *The Indoor League*, he had wanted to make a documentary about him. For Sid, he was the perfect blend of darter and man, and formed the template for others to follow: often drunk, lachrymose, rebellious and an outrageous show-off who couldn't give a toss. An embodiment of the rampant male ego Sid had admired astride the oche of his youth, bursting with working-class guts and regional pride.

He followed him around the exhibition circuit, trying and failing to match him pint for pint. Unlike Evans, Sid's lily liver prevented any descent into alcoholism. Two days on the drink and by the third he was sick as a dog. The thought of it would make him puke, and he needed several days to dry out before he could contemplate another drop. Just as well given his weakness for the booze; Evans had no such in-built deterrent.

But even through bleary eyes, what Sid witnessed enraptured him. At one event in Rochdale, Evans' arrival was greeted with the sort of throaty approval reserved for rock stars. Evans lived up to the billing by dressing in a white shirt and white flared trousers, like a miniature Elvis, running on best bitter rather than pills and burgers. On stage, he took and downed all comers, cracking lewd gags and threatening to beat up hecklers in between extravagant outshots.

By 1976, when Sid got permission to start making his film, Evans the Arrow had given up life on the dole and gone professional. He bought a Daimler Sovereign, hired a driver so he could concentrate on drinking, and toured the clubs, bars and holiday camps of England with Sid and his crew in tow. They captured him crying at the *News of the World* tournament when his best mate Leighton Rees' dreams of winning the tournament they all wanted were doused in the final; an international game in Somerset where Evans shone after necking six pints before hitting the stage and then threatening to hit everyone else; and a raucous exhibition in Liverpool where he beat the local hero on the bull.

The result was *The Prince of Dartness* (another of the countless nicknames Sid liked to give Evans). It was screened in the North-West in late 1976, but after a good response screened nationally the following year. While it proved the launching point for my father in the blossoming world of darts, it marked the high point of Evans' career. Despite the occasional flash of brilliance in the first few World Championships, he never fulfilled his potential and fell slowly, sadly and inexorably into alcoholic servitude and death at the age of forty-nine.

Sid felt buoyed: the film hadn't made him much money, but it had raised his flattened ego. Ray Colley was impressed and allowed him another shot at capturing the larger-than-life working men and women he revelled in. What followed was *The Landau Lads*, about the group of men and women who ferried holidaymakers along the Golden Mile in Blackpool. Once again it showcased his talent for bringing out the best in ordinary people who led sometimes extraordinary lives.

∽

If ever there was a moment of destiny in Sid's life it was when, while visiting the BBC in Manchester, he bumped into his old mentor, Donald Baverstock.

It was in the bar, naturally.

After leaving YTV in 1972, the Welshman had sought the job of controller of the BBC in his native land, but apparently the governors were discouraged by his 'casual behaviour' in the interview. After a couple of years in the wilderness, he was hired by BBC Manchester.

Baverstock had made his name as a producer on the *Tonight* programme and by encouraging programmes like *That Was the Week That Was* when he was boss of BBC1. In Manchester, he came up with the idea of *Terra Firma*, a magazine programme but with a definite intellectual bent. To this end, he contracted Alasdair Clayre, a fellow of All Souls, Oxford, and noted polymath but who had no track record on TV, and Nemone

Lethbridge, an upper-crust intellectual and one of the few women barristers at the time, who was banned from practising when it became known that she was married to Jimmy O'Connor, a convicted killer whose conviction was overturned many years later. Anchoring all this would be Ned Sherrin, the man responsible for *That Was the Week That Was*, more used to working with the likes of David Frost and Willie Rushton.

Donald managed to get Sid a staff job with the almost risible idea that he could somehow fit in with all of this. And yet he still managed to. By far his greatest success, perhaps of his entire career, was taking Nemone Lethbridge to Lynemouth to make a film of the men who scratched a living picking sea coal from the black beach.

Nemone had her young sons in tow, and so Sid took them to Dalton Avenue, where my granddad looked after them while their mother was filming. To his dying day, Bob never truly believed they were actually called Milo and Ragnar.

As Donald drove his Mercedes back each day from Manchester to Ilkley, he would offer Sid a lift. This gave him an excuse to stop off for a few pints at the Top House in Odsal Top, Bradford. He thought this was helpful, even though it often took Sid as long to get a bus into Bradford and back out to Pudsey as it did to take a train home from Manchester. However, Sid was in awe of Baverstock and didn't want to risk his wrath, so never told him the truth.

The show was a disaster, and its failure would ultimately cost Baverstock his job. 'I haven't often wondered what ever happened to Ned Sherrin, but now that I know, I'm going to try and forget,' wrote Jeffrey Bernard in his review of the programme in *The Spectator*.

Sid fared more successfully: he spent the best part of two decades in Manchester as a producer at the BBC.

~

One Saturday morning, a few months after he left the BBC, Baverstock turned up at our house in Pudsey when Sid was away filming. He was writing his memoirs, and he wanted Irene to type up some pages, remembering she had been a secretary but forgetting that was some time ago. He was lugging an ancient, heavy reel-to-reel tape recorder as he came through the front door. There was a surreal moment, watched by me, Charlotte and Irene, as Donald tried feverishly to plug the machine into various sockets in our sitting room until Irene realized its plug was a 13 amp round pin which worked in his eighteenth-century pile, Ilkley Hall, but not in our rewired Victorian Pudsey terrace. Needless to say, Irene had to change the plug.

Suddenly it was all too clear why he and Sid had been drawn to each other.

For the next two hours, he paced the sitting room listening to himself on tape and occasionally nudging Irene when he thought he'd made some good points in what seemed to her like a diatribe against the Beeb. Every time Charlotte and I tried to come in to ask Irene something, he'd shoo us away.

Finally, it was over. Irene changed the plug again, and Donald came out to use the toilet.

As he came downstairs, Charlotte, who was and still is scared of no one, said, 'Do you know what my brother calls you?'

'What?' asked Donald.

'He calls you Donald Babbasock.'

When he came to leave, I popped my head around the dining room door. He turned and fixed me with a steely glare. He had the face of a pugilist, and the air around him smelled of stale booze. I stood as still as a statue, sensing trouble.

He pulled on his coat, eyes still on me.

'Goodbye, Adolf,' he said and left.

~

The roots of a global darts tournament lay in Dino's barber shop in Chesterfield. Mike Watterson, a former car dealer from Derbyshire, was waiting for a trim. He had recently and successfully turned his hand to sport promotion after his wife Carole had been to see a play at the Crucible Theatre in Sheffield and was impressed with its hushed, intimate atmosphere. Mike was a champion amateur snooker player and was convinced it would work on a grander scale, and his wife suggested the Crucible as an ideal venue. Watterson paid the theatre manager £6,600 for two weeks' rental and assured the presiding snooker association they would make £17,000. They agreed, and history was made: the World Professional Snooker Championship is still held there to this day, and it's become one of the world's greatest sporting venues, a silent cauldron of tension and simmering drama.

Mike was still basking in the glow of the first tournament's success as he waited for his short back and sides and flicked through the pages of the *Derbyshire Times*. He shared a column with a darts player named John Lowe called 'The Way We Play It'. One week Watterson would discuss snooker; the next week

Lowe would write about his life as a darter. Lowe earned cash from the game: winning tournaments, performing exhibitions and playing money matches, such as one in 1975 where he and Yorkshireman Brian Langworth faced off against Evans and Leighton Rees in Wales for £6,000, which the Englishmen won. But like many others he still kept the day job. Only the brave few, among them Evans and Rees, had the courage or foolhardiness to go professional.

Watterson knew Lowe – he'd had some trophies engraved in Lowe's shop – and as he read about his travails, he had an idea. Haircut over, he went home and gave him a call.

'How many pros have you got?' Watterson asked.

'Not many,' admitted Lowe.

'I'm thinking about a World Professional Darts Championship, but I need more of you.'

The two mulled it over before they decided to call Olly Croft, the cocky cockney who had supplied Sid with darts players for *The Indoor League* and who had gone on to found the British Darts Organisation, rapidly becoming the strongest darts body in the land and soon to become the only darts body in the land through a combination of Olly's acumen and the success of televised darts.

There was no doubt the decision to ask Olly Croft and the BDO to help organize the first World Professional Darts Championship was the practical and right one. Without the best players, there was no chance the tournament would prosper. Much of its success was down to Olly Croft and his officials. But there is also no doubt that phone call from Mike Watterson was an important factor in helping make the BDO the most powerful darts organization in the world. Who knows what might have happened had Watterson and Lowe gone elsewhere?

The Heart of the Midlands nightclub was chosen as the venue; Embassy, the sponsors of the snooker championship, had agreed to put up the prize money of £10,500. Lowe, Evans and Rees were granted entry together with Scotsmen Rab Smith and Bobby Semple, inscrutable Swede Stefan Lord, the even more inscrutable Nicky Virachkul of the USA and two Australians, Barry Atkinson and Tim Brown. The last automatic place went to a brassy, beak-nosed twenty-year-old Londoner with almost cosmic self-belief, Eric Bristow. Other places would go to qualifiers.

There is a story that ITV were offered the chance of a similar event and turned it down, content with the tournaments they already screened. Ever since the riotously successful decision to show the 1972 *News of the World* finals, ITV had screened a number of other tournaments on *World of Sport*, which regularly bested *Grandstand* in the ratings. Unlike the BBC, where an executive had reportedly said, 'A dart will never be thrown on the BBC,' ITV could rightly claim to be the home of darts until its calamitous decision to stop *World of Sport*, and even beyond. It showed countless tournaments, nationally and regionally. Dave Lanning recalls with a mischievous grin how fellow ITV commentators like Brian Moore and Reg Gutteridge used to tease him about having to spend his time commentating in smoky halls in provincial towns, until their mocking turned to envy when the darts boom arrived, and he was sent to commentate in places like Honolulu and Las Vegas.

But in 1977, the BBC decided to cover darts, albeit on BBC2. Then, as now, there was a suspicion that it was more to do with the fact it would be a cheap way to fill the schedules at a time of year when much of the sporting programme was decimated by the weather. Whether or not that was the case, the pedigree of the team chosen to screen the tournament could not be doubted. Based in Manchester, they were led by a sharp, urbane and experienced producer named Nick Hunter, who had started his sports broadcasting career covering cricket in the mid 1960s and by 1977 was its producer, struggling, often vainly given the instinctive conservatism of BBC bosses, to drag the coverage into the modern era.

As a dry run, they scheduled a slot on *Grandstand* in December 1977 to screen the finals of the Treble Top Championship at the Park Hall Leisure Centre in Charnock Richard near Chorley, a three-a-side contest featuring teams from pubs who had won through a series of regional rounds, sponsored by Vernon's pools. It was hardly Lowe and Evans at their best, but it would be useful experience for the crew ahead of the World Championship.

Watterson arrived there early and met Hunter, who was setting up.

'Who's commentating?' he asked.

'David Vine,' Hunter said.

Watterson nodded approvingly. Vine was hardly a product of the taproom milieu of darts, but he was a pro and a mainstay of the BBC sports department. His presence meant the Beeb were taking it seriously.

'Oh, and a Geordie guy I work with,' Hunter added. 'Sid Waddell.'

~

Sid's odyssey from jobbing TV producer to the Geordie Lip had started a few months before his day of destiny in Chorley, in July 1977 at the Club Fiesta in Sheffield, which at Steeltown's height had attracted acts like the Jackson Five, Roy Orbison and the Beach Boys, but that weekend was hosting the British Intercounty darts finals. He had been working on a new show, *Roots of England*, when to his amazement Nick Hunter called to invite him for a voice-test.

According to Hunter, he knew and admired *The Indoor League*, and Sid's documentary about Alan Evans had convinced him that here was a man who understood darts players and might help squeeze every last ounce of drama from the action. It also helped that Sid was known to hang out in the bar, where he had been noticed for his love of tall tales and colourful vocabulary, not least by Hunter's PA Barbara Gibson, who often told him about a Geordie headcase who waxed lyrical about pub games while in his cups.

On a jaunt to London, as usual Sid contacted Dave Lanning for a tour of Soho's rococo, illicit drinking dens. They ended up in Acker Bilk's Capricorn Club, where Sid revealed the BBC's interest. He seemed nervous about it. But Dave agreed that his enthusiasm for pub sports and knowledge of the game was an excellent grounding, and Sid was reassured.

So it came to be that Irene drove a shaking, trembling, nervous Sid from Pudsey to Sheffield one Sunday morning a few days after Hunter's call. Irene parked and sat in the car reading the Sunday papers while Sid went inside to meet producer Keith Phillips. The players were warming up in traditional style by sinking a few pre-match pints, but Sid stayed on tap water. Phillips had a tape machine and a microphone, and he explained that he wanted Sid to crouch beside him, watch a match and offer a running commentary. Initially, he felt awkward, not least because the players wondered who the skinny curly-haired bloke gabbling into a microphone was, but they soon relaxed and so did my dad. His only problem was the volume of his voice: Sid was never a quiet man, his voice could rouse the dead, but he managed to maintain a volume that didn't disturb the players.

Afterwards, he and Phillips supped a pint, and the BBC man told him he had done well. A few days later, he was summoned to Hunter's office and told he had the job: first, a commentating stint for *Grandstand*, then in the New Year the first ever World Championship, to be screened on BBC2. Sid was left speechless, his excitement and panic only partly eased by the knowledge that neither event would be screened live and several bottles of red wine at the Midland Hotel.

Before his *Grandstand* appearance, Sid did what he could to swot up on outshots, trying to memorize the ways to finish from scores beneath 170 using an old *News of the World* chart produced to accompany a distant final. Language and words were Sid's strengths, and his struggle with figures and finishes would cause much angst and anxiety during his early years of commentary, where he thought his failure to remember the different ways to get out from 82 marked him as an idiot.

Many sleepless nights later, he arrived in Chorley eager to make his mark. Sadly, no footage of that *Grandstand* has survived, bar Frank Bough's avuncular introduction and Bob Wilson's *Football Focus*. Sid always claimed he called David Vine 'Dad' in the commentary, a shortening of 'Daddio', only for Vine to ask afterwards why he had insinuated he was an old man. Apart from that, he thought it had gone well, and as it was recorded the day before, he was able to watch it and wince the next day. But he knew the World Championship and five days of darts would be a sterner challenge, for both his larynx and his liver.

Johnny Dangerously

S ID WORKED IN television for almost forty-seven years, which is ironic because he hated watching television.

Given the choice between a TV drama or a book, there wasn't even a contest. I don't remember him watching much TV drama at all. This was in part because for much of his career the working days were so long, leaving before 7 a.m. and getting back between 8 and 9 p.m., that it didn't leave much time for TV viewing. But it was mainly because he didn't like watching it. I never asked if that was because he spent so long working behind the camera that he couldn't suspend disbelief, or if it was simply more fun to make programmes than watch them. I suspect the latter.

The only programme I remember him watching was *Auf Wiedersehen, Pet*, Clement and La Frenais' sublime comic drama about out-of-work Newcastle brickies forced to live and work in Germany. The idea was Franc Roddam's, who also came up with the idea of *Masterchef*. He met the two writers in LA and told them about the idea after a visit back to the North-East where he'd learned about Geordies going to Germany to help rebuild cities their bombs had flattened. 'I want to go and write it straight away,' Le Frenais said.

My dad and I loved it. For me it was a novelty to watch some-thing with him other than *Match of the Day*. Usually, I watched TV with Irene, while Sid buried himself in a book elsewhere. But Sid was entranced by the story and characters, delighted to see the sort of men he had grown up with and knew made flesh on screen. In particular, he loved the belligerent, feckless Oz, played by a raw Jimmy Nail. The two shared few similarities beyond a tendency to say 'bollocks' a lot, but Sid knew a well-drawn character when he saw one.

I reckon that deep down he wished he'd written it. The yearning for success, to make his mark, was still there, despite his growing cult status as a darts commentator. Ever since he was a child, he'd always written scripts and plays. That continued into adulthood but without him ever finding a strong idea. But watching *Auf Wiedersehen, Pet* made him more vigi-lant for those ideas that are right in front of you.

Beyond *Auf Wiedersehen, Pet* and *Match of the Day* though, I can't remember a single TV programme he watched other than to pass constructive comment on one of Irene's. Even late into life, when he didn't have to slog to and from Manchester each day and had weeks and months at home to himself, he didn't succumb to sitting in front of the box. There were occasional exceptions, the main one being the rare TV outings of Geordie comic Bobby Thompson.

Sid loved him; TV commissioning editors did not. He sham-bled on in an oversize, worn jumper, flat cap, fag held between nicotine-stained fingers. He spoke in a slow, thick pitmatic drawl, much like my granddad, and its impenetrability probably explained his infrequent TV appearances. He was the master of the mother-in-law joke, but there was a political edge my dad appreciated, which reflected the fact that Thompson was also raised in a mining community. 'I dreamt Margaret Thatcher had deèd . . . ah, but she went to heaven, an St Peter telt her, "Get away doon to Nick" . . . she went doon tae Nick, two-faced old fella . . . "Howay in, Meg." Ah, but he got fed up and he rung Peter. He says, "Get this woman out of here. She's only been here three days and she's closed three furnaces."'

The only TV he watched consistently was sport: US sports like baseball and NFL, cricket, rugby but mainly football, especially his beloved Toon.

Except they weren't really beloved. At the risk of exposing him as a fraud, he was no more than a fair-weather Newcastle supporter. Yes, he occasionally appeared in a Toon shirt on various TV programmes, and was often quoted as a fanatical Newcastle supporter in the press, or summoned on to local radio to offer a colourful opinion during one of the club's frequent meltdowns or crises. But the truth is he only ever attended one match at St James' Park in his life, and while he'd watch them on the TV, hands folded intently in front of his face, muttering 'bastard' whenever someone fouled a Newcastle player, he enjoyed a neutral game or Spanish football more. Sid the Toon Army fanatic became part of his growing public persona; meanwhile, Sid in his armchair in Pudsey was more enchanted by Barcelona.

Movies rarely appealed. Irene would occasionally drag him along to watch a film she was keen to see, but he could take or leave it. Videos were different. We were one of the first people we knew to get one. Unfortunately, we had a Betamax player, because Irene got one as a perk from YTV. She always insisted both the tapes and the machine were of superior quality. That might have been so, but it put us on the wrong side of the video-recorder wars. I'd walk into the video shop, eyeing enviously the rows and rows of VHS movies: all the *Rocky*s, all the *Star Wars*, all the films you could possibly want. Meanwhile, the Betamax section had one row, and all I can remember being available to rent was a Billy Connolly live concert and *Love at First Bite* with George Hamilton, which my sisters were able to recite by heart.

Irene relented and got a VHS within a year or so. Three years later, Sid had also worked out how to use it and would often be seen heading to the petrol station to rent a video. He nearly always watched horror.

His other favourite genre was foul-mouthed comedies: the more swearing, the better. You had not lived until you had watched such a film with Sid. I remember renting *Johnny Dangerously*, a so-so send-up of 1930s gangster movies, starring Michael Keaton as the titular hero. The film had some good gags and was mildly diverting, until the entrance of a character called Roman Moroni, an Al Capone-style hoodlum who is brought to trial by Johnny's attorney brother. His terrible Italian accent means he mangles every swear word he frequently utters. Sid loved emphatic, comedy swearing, so he started to giggle a little bit, aware of what was coming.

Moroni unfurls a piece of paper and addresses the court.

'I would like to direct this to the distinguished members of the panel: you lousy cork-soakers.'

Sid started to laugh, a wheeze that came from down in his guts. We all started to laugh too. You couldn't see him lose it like this and not laugh, regardless how lame the on-screen comedy.

'You have violated my fargin' rights.'

Sid was now leaning over in his seat, face creased, head nodding back and forth, emitting a high-pitched wheeze.

'Dis somanumbatching country was founded so that the liberties of common patriotic citizens . . . like me . . . could not be taken away by a bunch of fargin iceholes . . . like yourselves.'

By now, Sid was slapping the arm of his chair and shaking his head, tears streaming down his face. The wheeze had become a roar. It took at least ten minutes for him and us to calm down. The scene was moderately amusing; Sid's laughter was so infectiously hilarious you'd have to be made of stone not to join in.

A few years later, I watched the ten-pin bowling comedy *Kingpin* by the Farrelly Brothers with him, as a sort of background to his new career commentating on the sport for Sky. As Munson throws up in the background after having sex with his grotesque landlady to stave off eviction, she leans back in bed to have a post-coital cigarette.

'What is it about good sex that makes me have to crap?' she asks rhetorically, as Munson vomits copiously. 'I guess it's all that pumpin'. Pump and dump.'

By this point, Sid was laughing so hard I thought he might die of a heart attack there and then.

Waldorf and Statler

S ID WAS ALWAYS a twisted coil of nervous energy, so by the time of the first Embassy World Professional Championship in February 1978 he was almost sick with anxiety. The response to his commentary in Chorley had been good: Nick Hunter was pleased, and Mike Watterson thought his voice a perfect match for the action. But that was commentating on pub players. While Sid knew a number of the players involved in the Embassy from *The Indoor League* and trailing Evans around the circuit, that was as producer. Here he would be offering an opinion. The question he imagined them asking, directly to him or to each other, was 'What the hell does he know?' The likes of Evans and Bristow were not the type to take criticism from some Geordie gobshite who couldn't hit a treble if it was the size of a letterbox. It would take years for these nagging doubts to be hushed.

In order to avoid being shown up, every day he wasn't work-ing he went back to the Park Hotel in Pudsey to throw arrows. Not to improve – he was hopeless, though he could be lethal on double 13 – but to try to ingrain checkouts on to his brain. The championship was to be recorded, not shown live, which gave him a safety net, but the idea of dropping a clanger and being made to look a fool troubled him greatly. As he threw, he commentated on his play, which merely confirmed for the regulars what they already suspected: the Geordie bloke was certifiable.

He worried about his accent being too thick, but he was most tortured by his cough. Those close to Sid knew him by his cough: like a rough, phlegmy birdsong, it identified him even when he couldn't be seen. I could sometimes hear him coming down the street; the crackle of his cough as he got ready for work was my alarm call in the morning; and when he overdid the booze, it became more frenzied, often accompanied by spitting or worse. It was the consequence of a weak chest and the sooty, grimy air of his upbringing, and it got worse with nerves too. 'Nervous catarrh,' he called it. His fear was being on television 'while my catarrh gently seeps', he once said, but it was often no laughing matter.

By the time of 4 February 1978, the night before the first Embassy World Professional Championship, it was a wonder he could function as a human being. He checked in to the hotel and managed to steady his nerves with a few drinks. But the next day his stomach was churning, not helped by the knowledge that he and Vine would be commentating from a balcony – 'like Waldorf and Statler' – with no soundproofing. Sid's volume level on the darts was subterranean then compared to the hysterical peaks he would reach in his later career, but his voice was still loud enough to trouble some of the punters sitting nearby, who complained about the gabbling oddball with the microphone, and they didn't mean Vine.

The first night of coverage was inauspicious, to put it mildly.

The atmosphere at the Heart of the Midlands is like that of a mausoleum, and it clearly affects Bristow, the number one seed. He is beaten in a tortuous match with Conrad Daniels, a slow-coach US player, while Sid's commentary is staccato, stilted and hushed – all very BBC2. There are numerous references to the weights of each player's darts and to the prize of £3,000 for the winner. He allows himself one line, his first ever on-screen allusion: 'Conrad needs 48 for the biggest upset since the Walls of Jericho.' It's a rare flash of excitement. The second match sees the introduction of Evans and Alan Glazier, 'The Man in Black', and some excitement. The Welshman's vocal fans in the crowd wake everyone up: Sid, the crowd and the viewer.

That's if the viewer was still watching and had not disappeared in search of a sick bucket. The coverage is nightmarish: the cut between player and board is abrupt, the wide-angle camera lurches and wobbles and misses most doubles, while the tighter angle on the treble 20 misses every single cover shot. Every time Sid tries to predict an outshot he gets it wrong, while even Vine's links go awry. At one stage he informs us that Evans is 5–4 up and throwing for a match, only for us to see a leg at 4–2, which is won by Glazier. Vine then interjects to say, 'We've given you an extra game there. But now let's show you the final leg at 5–4 to Evans,' thereby revealing the result and ruining any tension. Once the game ends, there's a brief, unwitting cut to Vine in the studio, looking bemused. The viewer knew how he felt.

It was clear to all that the coverage did not work. Fixing it exercised almost everyone, in particular over how to solve the sudden switch between player and board that made for an unsettling, disorientating viewing experience, unsuited to a time slot when most people needed calm and flow to accompany their late-night cocoa. The solution was to split the screen, to allow the viewer to see the dart land in the board, while also allowing them to bear witness to the facial agony or ecstasy of the player in response. This simple technical solution changed darts from a sport that was difficult to capture to one made for the medium. There is no better place to watch darts than on television. There are times when the players or referee can't be certain if a dart is either side of a wire, but TV viewers almost always are; likewise, the crowd might not be aware when a player is suffering a mental collapse on stage, but the viewer will be.

The decision to split the screen has many fathers. Nick Hunter has claimed credit; Mike Watterson thinks David Vine was the one to suggest it; Sid said it was Nick and producer Ray Lakeland in concert; even Tony Green, who would soon join Sid as co-commentator, an experienced darts player, referee and MC, claimed the credit. He had been employed by the Beeb to perform the most crucial role in darts production: spotting. This involves telling the director which way the player might check out, so he can instruct the cameraman to cut to the right shot and avoid missing the dart. It is made more complicated by the fact that each player has a different way of finishing, depending on their favoured double or whim. Tony had been chosen to do the job that year, and he claimed in *Darts World* that he was the inspiration for the split screen that secured the game's television future. In the spirit of diplomacy, for which darts has *never* been known, let's say it was a team effort.

With such technical issues solved, the darts steadily grabbed an audience as the week progressed. There were reports of sports shops and manufacturers running low on stocks of darts and boards, as people took up the game, though that's probably an exaggeration given its graveyard slot in the schedule. But the audience was healthy, unlike the one in the hall. Watterson had hired a comedian to appear onstage after the darts to help lure people in, but even then the attendances were disappointing. The next tournament would be held at Jollees Cabaret Club in Stoke, a far more suitable venue.

The best match had been the quarter-final between Leighton Rees and his mate Evans, which is remembered for two things: Rees' ten-darter, which swung the momentum his way; and the same man downing half a pint in one gulp as Vine says disbelievingly, 'I think Leighton Rees is on his way to another record – that's his fifth pint already.' The comment caused consternation behind the scenes because the players thought Vine was sneering at them. From then on, there was no mention to be made of how much or how little players were swilling on the stage.

The only other footage that has survived is the final, won comfortably by Rees. The improvement five nights' experience has made is remarkable: the split screen works beautifully, the camera picks out most of the shots, even the crowd shows signs of life. Sid sounds more relaxed than he did at the start of the week but still subdued and constrained. There are no one-liners, no allusions, no hyperbole, just a whispered, almost mundane focus on the darts.

Perhaps it was exhaustion, because the twenty-four hours leading up to the final had been a saga. On the Thursday night after the darts, Sid was buoyed by praise and feeling good about himself. If there were two emotional states that were perilous for him, it was self-pity and self-congratulation, for both involved booze. That evening he supped several pints, then moved on to whisky and a few cigars. Even though he spent his life around smokers, because of his chest and mild asthma he was never a smoker himself: it made him ill, cigars especially.

The next morning, he had to get up at seven to work on his day job. Before he was allowed to take the darts gig, he had to promise his director on *Roots of England*, John Miller, that he would travel to Whitby, North Yorkshire, on the Friday to find some fishermen to film on a later trip. He calculated that if he left early enough, he would get there, complete the job and be back in time for the final. But he hadn't told Nick Hunter this. Nor had he factored in that he would have to complete a four-hundred-mile round trip with a hangover.

His train from Nottingham to York was at 7.30. He had no time to shave or wash, but he made it, and at York he felt well enough to risk breakfast. Then he took a taxi: not the cheapest option but the quickest. But as they drove over the North York Moors, the weather drew in and snow started to fall. It was slow going, and he arrived at 1.15 to meet his director, who, gallingly, had already found some fishermen who had agreed to take part, thus rendering the trip pointless. By 2 p.m., Sid was back in a taxi, but now the snow was fearsome. The cabbie expressed his doubts, fearing they might get stuck, but Sid waved a fiver under his nose, saying it was his if they got to York, and on that side of the Moors the weather was better. He made his train, had a brandy and a couple of sausage rolls to warm himself up, and walked back into the lobby of the Albany Hotel at 5.30 p.m., in good time but in soggy socks and clothes. That night he commentated in his bare feet.

In the final leg, as Rees neared victory, an excited edge creeps in to Sid's voice. But then, with Leighton needing 81, it starts to go wrong. Like the viewer at home, he relied on the pictures on the monitor in front of him. Leighton hits a single 19, then a 12, as the camera struggles to keep pace. 'What? I can't see,' Sid whispers, in the same exasperated tone he used at home when he couldn't get the contrast right on the TV, though, thankfully, employing fewer swear words. The mic picks it up, but luckily Leighton's last dart bounces out of the bull, injecting some drama, Sid comments on it, and his equilibrium is restored. Only briefly though, because as Rees returns requiring 50, Sid betrays his naivety by positing that he could hit the bull, which no top-class player would do with three darts in his hand. As if to rub it in, the Welshman hits 10 and then double top to win the World Championship. Again, it was a valuable lesson to listen to what Tony Green was saying to the director and then parrot that to the viewer.

Watching Rees hit the winning dart now, one expects Sid to explode into paroxysms of joy and verbal gymnastics. But we see Rees and Lowe shake hands, and the MC announces the winner. Sid remains silent. He told me that after the day he had had, with the stress of the long journey and then the nerves of the final, he felt more spent than either player. Next year, he vowed, he would make sure he had the whole week off.

In all, he felt it had gone well, but, despite assurances there would be more televised tournaments to come and he would be involved, he still viewed it as a temporary gig: something to supplement the day job. That insecurity was not eased when he learned that Tony Green would be promoted to the commentary box to share commentary duties with him in the future, as well as continuing to do the 'spotting'. Tony was a better darts player, more knowledgeable about the game, closer to the players and, as the son-in-law of the BDO honcho Olly Croft, better connected. Sid would need something to avoid coming across poorly in comparison.

The pages of *Darts World* carried little solace either. Describing Sid as a black mark 'on an otherwise superb darts series', William Cunningham, who, to make matters worse, was a fellow Geordie, added, 'When are TV darts presentations going to come up with someone to leave the calculating to the players?'

Cunningham's letter marked the beginning of an annual tradition in *Darts World*: the post-Embassy letter slagging off Sid. He was a sensitive soul, and it would take some time for these jibes to stop hurting.

'I'm Jack'

To BE A YOUNG child in West Yorkshire in the late 1970s was to be aware of evil. You knew for certain that the Bogeyman existed. The days were fine, but the twilight world seethed with menace and danger: somewhere out there in the night, down that dark ginnel, lurking on a patch of wasteland, behind the trees in the parks, driving that solitary car with its headlights like two eyes of a monster, was a demon. His name was the Yorkshire Ripper.

I don't remember anyone telling me what he had done or who he was. They didn't need to. With three sisters and a step-mother around me, the fear seeped in by osmosis: whispered conversations that stopped when you entered the room; forced smiles that were meant to reassure but did anything but; the TV turned off halfway through news reports; frantic discussions about journeys and how people might get from A to B; the anxious, panicked glances at the clock when it reached the time for someone to be at home and the sigh of relief when they walked through the door.

There was not a woman young or old in West Yorkshire and beyond who felt safe when the Ripper was at large. None went out alone after dark if they could help it. Every woman seemed to have a story of walking home, hearing or sensing footsteps behind, feeling their heart quicken. Harmless men appeared as potential killers, while every car that slowed down or pulled in to park brought with it unease.

For a child, the atmosphere was febrile, the foreboding oppressive and the nightmares endless. Who was this maniac?

Then one day we knew. He had a voice. I remember the news reports: grim-faced coppers sitting in silence as the tape of his lilting, taunting voice rang out: *I'm Jack. I see you're having no luck catching me. I have the greatest respect for you, George, but Lord, you're no nearer catching me now than four years ago when I started . . .*

The sinister drawl of the Ripper's voice electrified the whole area – the demon had been made flesh. It was played repeatedly on the news, in the hope someone would recognize it, and then replayed over and over in a million bad dreams. Everyone believed it belonged to him, the beleaguered, exhausted West Yorkshire police force included. They seized upon it. In his arrogance, his desire to brag and tease them, they believed he had handed them a lead. There was no doubt the voice on the tape belonged to the murderer.

And the voice on the tape was a Wearside one, which sounded like Sid's to those unaware of the nuances of North-East accents.

In 1979, while he was in Stockton commentating on a team event for the BBC, Sid was called by the police and asked to present himself for an interview with two West Yorkshire detectives the next morning. It did nothing for his state of mind, given that he was already suffering a crisis of confidence over his commentary, but the next day he met two detectives at his hotel, with two BDO officials complete in maroon blazers as his witnesses in case the cops got heavy, and was interviewed in a conference room.

Sid had drunk late into the night before with David Coleman and Tony Green, and, as always when hungover, he was skittish and tightly wound. The cops must have wondered why. One of the detectives told him that a number of people had contacted them to suggest his voice matched the one on the 'I'm Jack' tape, and they were obliged to make inquiries. Then he was given a number of dates, when the Ripper had struck, and asked to supply his whereabouts for each one. Sid consulted his pocket diary. On a few of those dates, he had been in and around the Leeds and Bradford area where the victims had been found. No surprise – he lived nearby and was known to frequent the pubs of both cities. The detectives gave away no emotion, but Sid started to feel uneasy.

Next he was asked why he kept details of his movements. Sid explained that he reclaimed expenses from the BBC and needed to make a note of all his journeys. Again there was no response, but Sid's sense of dread grew. What were they building up to, he wondered.

'What kind of car do you drive?' was the next question.

'I don't,' replied Sid.

'What do you mean?'

'I can't drive,' he told them. 'I took lessons, but I was rubbish. I never passed my test. I take public transport.'

The two detectives looked at each other. The Ripper had to be able to drive in order to cover the distances he did. Survivors and witnesses had offered descriptions of cars driven by the suspect. Accent or not, they knew that the most notorious serial killer of modern history did not travel to and from the scenes of his brutal crimes by bus.

'Why didn't you tell us that?' one of the detectives asked with incredulity.

Sid shrugged. 'You never asked, kidda.'

That wasn't the end of it though. Some time later, on a day when he wasn't feeling well and was at home, he made an appointment to see the doctor. Within a couple of hours, two policemen turned up on our doorstep.

'Oh God, not again,' sighed Sid.

'What do you mean?' asked Copper No. 1.

'I've already been grilled by Teesside police. They seemed convinced I wasn't the Ripper.'

It was obvious that the doctor's receptionist had contacted the police because she thought she recognized the accent. The two policemen took a few notes and left. This was a small example of the utter chaos surrounding the police investigation, and how hundreds of Geordies living around Leeds and Bradford were tainted by suspicion.

~

In 1980, the Ripper murdered Jacqueline Hill on a plot of barren land behind the Arndale shopping centre in Headingley, a few miles from our house. Unlike most of his other victims, Hill was not a prostitute. She had been walking home when the Ripper drove past her, stopped his car, watched her go by and then attacked her with a hammer. A few months later, I was in Headingley with Sid when we walked near the site on Alma

Road where she was found. I remember staring at it with awe. It seemed to exude evil, as if the horror of what had happened there had been imprinted upon the landscape.

Following her murder, the streets of Leeds and Bradford and their suburbs were ghost towns after dark. For those who were forced to go out by circumstance, the uncanny, eerie atmosphere of those deserted streets seemed like some post-apocalyptic world. The early winter of 1980–81 was shrouded in cold and malevolence and seemed to last for ever.

Then, in January of 1981, the police found him: the Ripper had a name – Peter Sutcliffe. There was a pause as people could not quite believe he had been caught, then came an outpouring of fervent relief when it became clear he was the killer, like the feast at the end of a fast. Spring came, and with it Sutcliffe's life sentence; after the fear-induced hibernation, everywhere seemed to hum with people and energy. They were safe once more. *We* were safe once more. But no woman or child of that area and era ever hears footsteps behind them in the dark and doesn't recall those years of fear.

The law eventually also caught up with Wearside Jack, who made the hoax recording that derailed an already shaky investigation. Sid was one of forty thousand men interviewed as a result of this deception, and a million quid was spent on trying to find the man behind it. While the police searched down this blind alley, three more women were murdered. The culprit, John Humble, was caught when police reviewed the case in 2005 and extracted some DNA from the gum seal of one of the hoax letters he posted to the murder team. He pleaded guilty to perverting the course of justice and was sentenced to eight years.

The First Days of Darts

B Y THE TIME of the final of the 1979 World Championship, Sid was determined to change his approach to commentary. Throughout his professional life he had tried to innovate and imprint his personality on his work rather than follow the path well worn. He was learned, widely read, with a brain full of history and literature. Rather than trying to predict outshots, or puncture the play with obvious clichés about players needing to respond or digging deep or feeling the pressure, he decided he needed to add more colour.

Irene had driven to Stoke to join him for the final weekend of the 1979 championship at Jollees, a smoky, beer-soaked den with a guttural roar that provided the ideal backdrop and soundtrack. John Lowe and Leighton Rees were about to repeat their contest of the year before, and Sid was prowling the hotel room like a dog in search of a Bonio as Irene read the papers and worked her way through a complimentary pack of Embassy cigarettes. It had been a good week, and his commentaries had reflected it. He sounded more assured, more like Sid: there were references to treble 20 as the 'red bit' and a cry of 'on the wiy-ah!' whenever a player came close to a double, both of which would become staples of his repertoire.

The TV was on, and it was showing the return of the Ayatollah Khomeini from exile to rapturous scenes in Tehran, one of Sid's old stomping grounds. Sid watched for a few seconds and cleared his throat. 'If Lowe wins this, there'll be a reception in Clay Cross like the Ayatollah Khomeini had come to town.'

Irene pulled down her newspaper. 'You cannot possibly say that!'

Sid did not respond.

Later that evening, she was in the sponsors' room as the final neared its end. Lowe was running away with it 4–0 and came to the board needing double 10 for the title. He took it out with his first dart, grinned and turned to shake his opponent's hand. Those around Irene had paused briefly for the climactic moment but then returned to their conversations. Irene was chatting with Celia Dyke, the wife of Peter, Imperial Tobacco's chief executive, as Sid, unlike the year before, toasted the victor.

'The grin of the champion. The new champion being congratulated by the old. And there'll be a reception in Clay Cross as if the Ayatollah Khomeini had walked into town.'

Irene stopped talking. She turned to a group of men near the TV.

'Did he just say what I thought he said?' she asked.

The men were laughing. 'Yes!'

She shook her head. Not for a second did she imagine Sid would say the line he had rehearsed in the hotel room. What had he done?

Nothing bad was the answer. Sid feared a bollocking or some kind of admonishment, but instead Nick Hunter praised both the line and his overall commentary. It went down well with

TV reviewers and critics, as did the tournament. The only dissenting voice was Patrick Collins, who, as Sid pointed out, never missed an opportunity to knock the sport. Rather prissily, he described the championship as 'a tawdry circus'. Sid loved journalists and made time for and gave quotes to them all – local or national, experienced or cub, radio, TV or print. But the only one I ever remember him disliking was Patrick Collins, because of his disregard for the sport, the players and its fans. Sid could forgive many flaws, but he hated snobbery.

The week was memorable for many reasons. David Coleman presented, adding some old-school gravitas and indicating how seriously the BBC were now taking the darts, despite the odd grumble from West London about why they were showing fat boozy men chain-smoking and guzzling ale, while intermittently flinging bits of metal at a mat. Bristow and Evans produced a match of seething animosity that made for compelling TV, culminating in a worse-for-wear Evans slagging off the BDO in his post-match interview, which led to him being banned for a year for bringing the game into disrepute and in turn provided Sid with one of his favourite darting stories. 'How can Evans *bring* the game into disrepute?' a pissed Welsh darts fan asked him later. 'We've always been in disrepute!'

~

On the night before the championship started, Sid arrived at the Crown and Anchor pub in Longton, Stoke, in the driving rain. He shivered in the cold, pulling his coat across his chest, passing a short fat man with a mullet and tatty anorak gazing up at the pub sign. Sid ignored him and hurried in, pushing his way through the boozy throng to the bar where Cliff Lazarenko was doling out pints to help the landlord cope with the crushing, thirsty mass. Sid waited patiently until he was about to be served, when suddenly he was pushed aside. He turned, half in anger: it was the chubby bloke from the pavement outside, clutching a battered miniature suitcase that held most of his worldly possessions, a half-eaten cheese roll hanging forlornly from his pocket. Sid was about to protest, but something wild in the man's eye told him that would be unwise.

Big Cliff clapped his hands together.

'What do you want, Jocky?'

Thus was Sid's first meeting with his favourite darts player of them all, the Scot who stole his heart: Jocky Wilson.

Jocky came from nothing. He and his brother grew up in an orphanage. He could not read or write. The only thing he could do was play darts. It wasn't a sport to him; it was a means of survival. Tournaments were good because they meant money if he won. But his bread and butter was to play games for cash to feed his wife and kids and keep him in beer and fags and dentures. Unlike his darts, Jocky was toothless. Sid visited him in his tiny flat in Kirkcaldy once, where his wife Malvina made them mince and tatties, washed down with copious tins of strong lager. Sid politely finished his plate. Jocky didn't, leaving his false teeth on a pile of cold congealed ground beef and potatoes.

'That's disgusting,' said Sid.

'I know,' said Malvina. 'That man never finishes a meal!'

Back in Longton, Jocky offered to play Tony Green for money. The game went on for most of the night and the stakes rose. It was 2 a.m., and Sid was keen to get back to the hotel to sleep because it was an afternoon start the next day. He called a taxi, and when it arrived, he went over to tell Tony Green, unaware the match was reaching its denouement.

'Shut yer fucking mouth when the game's on, Geordie,' Jocky roared.

It was an inauspicious start, but over the years the two became close, and Sid revelled in Jocky's success. Sid even ghosted a quick cash-in autobiography. He loved how Jocky had overcome a terrible, abusive upbringing to become one of the world's best. It was fairytale stuff. Sid once told me that Jocky wept uncontrollably when Bobby George, whom he partnered in exhibitions and shared prize money with, bought him a silver chain. It was the first gift anyone had given him in his life. Sid loved the fact he wore his heart on his sleeve with every dart, his broad beaming face a canvas of joy and agony, and his ability to surf the emotion of the crowd, to bait or whip it into a frenzy. He was flawed, of course: he was often drunk, often aggressive, though rarely physically so. But that all added to the package in Sid's view. Shortly after Jocky's death in 2012, but sadly soon before his own, Sid wrote his obituary for the *Sun* and signed a deal to write the unexpurgated story of Jocky's remarkable rise and fall, an epic, cinematic tale of rags and fags to riches and back to rags and fags again.

But it was never written.

~

If darts boomed during 1979, with more televised events on both ITV and the BBC, it exploded in 1980 after the world final between the game's two greatest showmen, Bobby George and Eric Bristow. Both were young, both were cocky, both thrived on stage. Then as now, so many darts players were capable of throwing world-class darts in untelevised tournaments 'on the floor'; only a fortunate few were able to reproduce that form under lights on the stage, in front of the cameras. Bristow and George were two of them. Their match, shown live on the BBC, is widely credited with cementing the popularity of darts in the public consciousness.

Bristow oozed arrogance, sneering, with a grin and a sharp word never far away. Sid often felt the stab of his tongue for some perceived slight. At one World Championship, Bristow hectored him across the car park for not tipping him to win in his column in the tournament programme. As Sid said, Bristow was a proud man who looked for disrespect and was often quick to find it.

George on the other hand was more clubbable and jovial, a gravel-voiced wideboy with charm to spare. Sid loved the flash and the bling: the jewellery, the Rolls Royce and sequinned shirts, 'like an explosion in a paint factory'. He once booked Bobby to perform on a Sunday evening at a benefit for the Yorkshire cricketer Colin Johnson, who also played at our local club, Pudsey St Lawrence. He arrived at our house in Pudsey at teatime, with his MC, Martin Fitzmaurice, known as Fatzmaurice for his generous girth, and a driver. Irene was making Sunday dinner for the seven of us, the only one she cooked all week and the only one that we would sit together to eat. It was often the only time we sat together at all. Irene was now a producer and director at Yorkshire Television and would be the first to admit that at this point cooking did not play a pivotal role in her life. She rotated three dishes weekly: chicken, beef, casserole. We prayed for a chicken week, and that was one. Two fine plump birds, roasted to perfection, with roast potatoes, mash and three veg. We had all been out for the afternoon, but like homing pigeons we headed for home at 5.30, lured by the rare scent and promise of home-cooked food.

Except that week we were faced with bare carcasses and the offer of a cheese sandwich. Bobby, Fatz and the driver had eaten it all: both chickens, all the veg, probably the plates. There wasn't a scrap left. As my stepbrother Nick would say, 'Bobby George ate my Sunday dinner. And Lucy's . . . and Emma's . . .'

∽

But that was in the future. Back in 1980, that final was the first I remember watching on television, and I was cheering for Bobby. There was something too angular, too confrontational about Eric for a seven-year-old boy to warm to. I was in awe of Kenny Dalglish and his ruddy-cheeked grin of delight whenever he scored. Snarling, smoking Bristow and his cultivated air of cockiness was more pantomime villain. But Eric didn't want to be loved; he wanted to win. More often than not, he did.

It had the feeling of an event. Two contrasting characters, live on television, in front of a raucous, partisan crowd, chanting 'Bobby George!' or 'Bristow!' at each other, through clouds of billowing fag smoke. I remember vividly how they entered the stage, emerging from a small door to a vast growl of expectation from the crowd. 'It's like having a ringside seat at the Coliseum,' Sid said as the cameras surveyed the baying crowd.

The match lived up to his rhetoric: each man trading sets until George blinked first, mopping sweat from his face while Bristow barely raised a bead. He won a memorable, rollicking encounter 5–3 after George bust his attempt at double 18 to level at 4–4, and then planted a kiss on his opponent's cheek.

The game is etched into darting folklore. And Sid found the words to match. If 1979 had seen him grow in confidence, then 1980, like Bristow, saw him near his best. He was now the voice of darts, an impression further ingrained by the famous *Not the Nine O'Clock News* darts sketch that followed in 1980, where Fat Belly and Even Fatter Belly down single pints, double and treble spirits while Rowan Atkinson imitates Sid's Geordie accent.

Some in the darts world were appalled. It reduced them to a laughing stock, they claimed. Bobby George voiced a protest that both men in the sketch were fat, yet he and Eric were not. An accurate observation, if one that missed the point. The sketch was a sign of the sport's growing success, and it would do wonders to increase the game's appeal rather than harm it. People tuned in to see what the joke was about and were soon sucked in by the unfolding drama and high-tension machismo. Sid would often be quoted in high dudgeon in the press, saying the sketch was an insult that devalued the athleticism and the skill of the players. But he did not believe a word of it; he knew that kind of publicity was not up for sale. All was good: darts was immensely popular, and people were doing impressions of him on prime-time TV.

The features started to roll in. When the hacks and colour men realized Sid was a Cambridge graduate with a flair for words, they flocked to him. He became the sport's and the players' foremost publicist and PR man. He'd do publicity at the drop of the hat and next day buy five copies of the paper. He revelled in it, both for his own ego but also because these unsung men, the kind of guys who never made the posh papers or the TV, were being hailed as heroes.

This was the Golden Age of darts. New televised tournaments appeared each week, new sponsors, increasing prize money, a mass of publicity, all helped by the sprawl of characters at the top end of the game. Bristow and George, stone-faced John Lowe, Cliff Lazarenko, who would give Even Fatter Belly a run for his money, certainly at the bar, Rees and Evans, 'The Man in Black' Alan Glazier, studious Dave Whitcombe and, of course, Jocky.

After Bristow won again in 1981, Jocky took the 1982 crown. It was a hugely popular victory, not least with Sid, who struggled to contain both his bias and his emotions. I can hear the nerves as Jocky takes a few seconds to gather himself before throwing for the match; fag in hand, he slaps his hip in self-encouragement. When he takes out double 16 for the title, there is a fatherly pride and joy in Sid's voice. 'Jocky wins. Lowe congratulates him. The victor takes the plaudits . . . and the tears aren't far off, the tears of pride. They'll be singing, they'll be Highland flinging all over Scotland for this lad. Didn't he do well? He kisses the board . . . Champion.' He is on the verge of tears. No victory for any player, before or since, meant more to him.

'I've Seen Nothing Like It
In Me Life!'

REGARDLESS OF THE heights previously scaled by darts, the 1983 Embassy World final was its zenith. One of Sid's favourite lines of his own came late in his career, after he re-read *The Snows of Kilimanjaro* by Ernest Hemingway. In this story, based on fact, the frozen carcass of a leopard is found at 24,500 feet, close to the western summit of Kilimanjaro, referred to as 'Ngaje Ngai' (House of the Gods) by the locals. Sid loved the idea of a snow-topped mountain in Africa ('a brilliant paradox, kidda') but also that, to this day, no one knows what the leopard was doing at such a high altitude. What was it striving for? Next time he commentated on Phil Taylor's excellence, he said, 'He's like that leopard on Kilimanjaro.' Meaning: he had scaled peaks of brilliance never previously thought possible in his search for perfection. Of course there's a chance his audience might not have read the short stories of Hemingway and didn't have the foggiest what he was on about.

But the Deller–Bristow final of 1983 was darts' frozen-leopard moment. It's hard to believe that any other match would imprint itself on the nation's psyche like the one between milk-drinking twenty-three-year-old Keith Deller, a 66–1 qualifier who was so proud of his recent England selection that he wore his red and white international outfit all week, and Bristow, the Crafty Cockney, who had sailed through the week seemingly unstoppable. Eric was only three years older than the fresh-faced Deller, but his worldly mien, the swagger and strut, and the ever-present cigarette made him appear to be from another generation, if not another world.

Deller had been on the circuit for a couple of years and was known and rated. En route to the final, he had defeated former champions John Lowe and Jocky Wilson, but no one gave him a chance. 'He's not the underdog, he's the underpuppy,' Sid told viewers. And he was playing 'Stoke Newington's answer to Attila the Hun'. It seemed a mismatch. But Sid also predicted that for all his boyish bounce, Deller would not wilt under Bristow's onslaught, and, for once, a prediction of his proved right.

The final was screened on *Grandstand* at teatime on a Saturday and drew 8.3 million viewers, comfortably the greatest televised audience for a darts match before or since. The scene was set for Sid after a tough week: he had been afflicted by an attack of gout, which caused him agony but eased as the week went on. Then, after the semi-finals, he made the mistake of socializing with the snooker player Ray Reardon and drank more pints than was wise: even worse, he smoked cigars. On top of an already bibulous week, his body rebelled and he felt terrible. The headache was bad, but the wheeze and cough were hellish. His voice was ravaged. He was about to broadcast live to the nation, and he feared a coughing fit or worse.

As it was, his straining voice stood up to the early part of the game, and his commentary is assured and confident. Deller showed he was in no mood to be bullied by Bristow and eased into a 2–0 lead, then 3–1. Tony Green replaced Sid for a few sets as Bristow fought back to 3–3, only for Deller to move within a set of victory at 5–3. He missed six agonizing darts at a double to win the title, and Bristow stepped in. Soon it was 5–5, and Deller looked broken. By now Sid was back in the commentary box, apparently to call Bristow's third World Championship and the young man's agony at a golden opportunity missed.

What followed was one of the finest ten minutes in British sporting history and, in my opinion, the finest commentary of my father's life. A night on the panatellas with Ray Reardon did him the world of good: his overtaxed, keening voice is the perfect bridge between the taut drama on screen and the tumultuous, ecstatic crowd.

Eric takes the first leg against the throw, and it seems all over bar the boozing. Sid is announcing Deller's requiem. 'His parents should be proud of this lad. He came here this week and has played brilliantly.' The jig was up. Or was it? Deller, his chalked dart tips smudging and spattering the 20 bed, would not give up. Bristow threw what Sid called 'a couple of daft ones', and Deller, as he had done all week with style, took out a high finish – 121. The crowd went into raptures. 'I don't quite believe this, but those lot obviously do. One apiece in the decider.'

Deller, now glugging lager not milk, drinks as Eric casts him a rueful sidewards glance, some of the chippy, chirpy light in his eyes dulled. He hasn't been able to throw the underpuppy off the scent all game, and he knows it. Deller throws first in the third leg as the crowd struggle to maintain order. After back-to-back 140s, Sid cries, 'The crowd emoting!', but he's wise enough to let the shouts and roars punctuate the darts as pandemonium erupts when Deller takes out 68 to go within a leg of victory. 'They're knocking the floorboards off, they're so excited,' says Sid. Deller offers a dopey smile to someone in the crowd. 'And that young lad's still grinnin'!'

But Brissy has the darts and a 140 gives him the edge. One dart of Deller's slides into the treble 1, but the other two are perfect: 123. Eric hits a solid ton. The pressure is on the younger man. He's up to it: another 140. 'He's got an arm as true as Alan a Dale,' Sid intones slowly, referencing one of Robin Hood's Merry Men, not an obscure Irish darter. The excitement has broadened Sid's accent as surely as a pint in the Hot L. 'What a throwah, Dellah.'

But another 140 maintains Eric's advantage. A tiebreaker and sudden death seem certain. After Deller hits 100, Eric sits on 121, the Ipswich man on a tricky 138. Eric hits single 17, treble 18 to leave a shot at the bull. But he famously, unforgettably, unforgivably chooses to hit single 18 to leave his favourite double 16, thinking he will get a chance to take it out at his next visit, even though Deller has been checking out from a ton plus all week. 'Played the percentage shot!' notes Sid, with more than a hint of surprise.

Up steps Deller. One hundred and thirty-eight is not a straightforward shot at all, as anyone knows who has heard Bristow talk about this before. 'One up there,' he says, pointing to the treble 20, 'one over there,' he says, pointing to treble 18, 'and one back over there,' he says, pointing to double 12. All over the board. Had Deller been left on 140, two treble 20s and then tops, or 136, two 60s and double 8, there's no way Eric would have laid up. But no one knows finishes better than Eric Bristow: he can recite every combination of every outshot from every conceivable score quicker than a computer. More than that, he knows exactly how each player likes to finish. He knew that Deller wouldn't go two treble 20s and double 9. No one goes for double 9 if they can help it. It's in a horrible part of the board, and if you miss inside the wire, you leave yourself an odd number and one less dart at a double for the next throw. Eric made a mistake, but it was his underestimation of his opponent's mettle that was the error, not a fault in logic.

'Dangerous by Bristow; he's banking on Deller not doing this,' says Sid as Deller plants the first dart in the left-hand part of the 60 bed.

'But the shot's on for the title!'

The crowd seems to have fallen silent with disbelief as Deller hits treble 18, shown in wide shot.

'Double 12 for the title!'

The camera zooms in. Deller takes it out, just bending the lower wire at the heart of the bed.

The crowd roars as if it was a late winner at Wembley. Referee Freddie Williams screams, 'YEEEEEEEEEEEEEEE-AAAAAAASSSSSSSS!' Deller turns and leaps, arms raised, and then offers Eric his hand. 'GAAAAAAAAMMMMMEEEEE...' shouts Williams.

Sid breaks in, his voice close to cracking: 'I am tellin' ya, I'm tellin' ya, I've seen nothing like it in me life! Keith Deller of Ipswich! Twenty-three-year-old! He had to qualify to get here. Bristow did a percentage shot . . . Deller did the business. He's now the world champion. A freak-out here at Jollees. A freak-out! Wondrous darts.'

People across the country yelled with joy, fell out of their seats with surprise, danced a jig or spilled their tea or ale. It was the sporting surprise of the year and a darts match for the ages. Sid always regretted knackering his voice the night before, but it gives those final lines, his rising intonation as he strains to be heard over the melee of the crowd, an incredulity and emotion that perfectly fitted the bedlam in the crowd and the commotion on stage. Darts had its greatest hour, and Sid had his finest commentary.

Creatures of the Pub

SID, AS DAVE LANNING told me, was a creature of the pub. Much of his life was spent in them. When lonely, he went there for company. When happy, he went there to celebrate. And with friends, he went there to socialize. He went after work, during and occasionally before. He went there for a quick pint and to fill long hours. He went there to dull his brain but also for inspiration: some of his best ideas came in pubs, while many of his breaks and opportunities arose from meetings there, chance or otherwise. And he preferred dank, carpeted backstreet boozers to gentrified floorboarded gastropubs. I'm not sure he saw the point of food in pubs, beyond nuts, crisps and scratchings – 'Pudsey tapas' as he named it. And of course, many of the men he worked with were fellow graduates of the taproom.

Sid believed that you could tell a lot about a man from the way he behaved in a pub. This etiquette was passed on to me as law. First and foremost, you bought your round. If you were drinking quicker than others, you didn't tap the table anxiously and break the natural drinking rhythm of others, you bought yourself an 'in-betweener'. But neither did you nurse a drink for hours: if others were ready, and it was your round, you bought it, whether your pint was finished or not. At the bar, if others had been waiting longer, you gave way. You never, ever held others up and paid for a drink with plastic, and, if you were a regular, you made sure you bought the barmaid or barman one at the end of the evening. And if you were pissed, you went home. The latter was the only one he struggled to live up to, as do I, come to think of it. And I have used a card to buy drinks. Forgive me, Father, for I have sinned.

Throughout his life, wherever Sid went he made friends and few enemies. When recalling Lynemouth, school, Cambridge, Durham, Yorkshire TV, the BBC or darts, there was always a mate involved in his stories and scrapes. Dick Bramley, Charles E. Hall, John Wilford, J.B. Meade – names of men I barely knew but who were made flesh in Sid's shaggy-dog stories. Yet he never seemed to keep in regular touch with any of them, apart from Dave Lanning. In later life, he would be in touch with them sporadically, almost by accident, a chance meeting in a bar or on a train somewhere, a wedding and then more often a funeral. But he had always had the pub and its denizens.

In particular, Sid knew the joy of the pub at 4 p.m. The lull after the lunchtime crowd has gone, before the after-work crowd invades. The stillness; the tick of the clock; the pull of the pint; and uninterrupted access to the pool table. It's a love I share: the illicit thrill giving the beer an added bite, slipping down all too easily as you realize the world is still at work and here are you on the skive. Stepping out blinking into the sunshine, watching people schlep past, wondering if there is a chance to sink another somewhere else.

Almost every weekday he was at home and, fit and able in the last twenty years of his life, he would write and read and then at 4 p.m. head to the pub. For many years, his destination was the White Cross, where he played pool with a maths teacher who dived in there after school with a raging thirst. Sid called him 'the Professor', and they would play four matches, have three pints, and then Sid would walk home. When at home, I often joined them. The Professor was a bit addled by booze but basked in Sid's fond ribbing. He once fluked a double. 'Hypotenuse said that was impossible,' Sid said. 'But he never played here,' he added, to the Professor's professional amusement.

The White Cross went to seed and so did the Professor: he ended up doing his post-school drinking in Pudsey's Conservative Club. There was no way on earth Sid would enter a Conservative Club unless it was to lay the dynamite to demolish it, so that was the end of their friendship. The White Cross, like the Professor, is no more.

Sid changed his local to the Mason's Arms at the bottom end of town, a small pub so tatty and old-fashioned that none of the young drinkers who blighted other Pudsey pubs would go near it. So of course Sid loved it. His pool companion was Keith, who lived across the road. Sid called him the Professor too, though with more veracity this time: he taught history at the University of Huddersfield. They had much in common, not least that neither of them drove and both relied on wives and public transport to get them about. My dad's visits to the Mason's would coincide with Keith's bus dropping him off, and they'd shoot pool and sip pints. Then Keith had a minor heart attack, and so my dad played pool with the barmaid – 'She is shit hot,' he told me – until Keith's health recovered enough for him to return, although now he drank healthy red wine and Sid drank halves, as if trying not to make him feel bad.

Sid fed Keith yarn after yarn. He once told him that he hoped his later life would be turned into a film and that Keith, a short chubby man in specs, would be played by Dustin Hoffman. The Mad Professor – Sid appended the adjective presumably to distinguish him from the other professor, even though Keith was as sane as they come – once made a seven-cushion escape from being snookered that so staggered Sid he ended up recounting it to Steve Davis during his foray into pool commentary. 'No professional would try such a shot,' replied Davis. In Sid's retelling, Keith twinkling with pride, the six-times world snooker champion wasn't criticizing but intimating that no earthly man would have the gumption to try something so audacious. There was another connection between them: Keith supervised Patrick Chaplin's thesis on darts. He's now Dr Patrick Chaplin (Dr Darts) and the only man alive who knows more about darts than Sid did.

Sid made no close friends in the thirty-seven years he lived in Pudsey, but hundreds of acquaintances. Irene tells a story of their weekly shop to Asda only a few years after we had moved in with her and Nick. As they walked up and down the aisles, Sid pushing the trolley, she noticed him nodding at various other men trailing behind their wives.

'Who was that?' she asked.

'Stan. Drinks in the Golden Lion.'

Another middle-aged man Irene didn't recognize passed and nodded.

'Graham, Butcher's Arms,' Sid explained.

They carried on. 'Gary, the Black Bull.' 'Stewart, the White

Cross.' 'Dennis, the Park Hotel.' There seemed to be no pub regular Sid didn't know.

'Bloody hell,' said Irene. 'You've lived here five minutes and you know more people than me.' A few foreign postings aside when her father was in the RAF, she had lived in Pudsey all her life.

A well-upholstered gent with florid cheeks walked by with a cheery 'Aye up, Sid.'

'Trevor,' my dad told Irene as the man disappeared into frozen foods. 'Any pub you care to mention.'

Jollees

GLEN FREEMAN AND I stood in the driving rain in January 1985 outside Jollees, a nondescript sixties building tagged on to a bus station that hinted nothing of the joys within. Outside, it was dark and the streets were silent and still, as if all the town's population was inside. I was twelve. As we were taken in through the front entrance, past blue-rinsed women dressed in crimplene and selling programmes, I not only crossed into the world of darts but into the world of men. We walked through a set of double doors into a pungent smog of smoke and ale. Rows and rows of men in a run-down cabaret club, wearing cardigans, chuffing on fags and pipes, trays of drinks both full and empty strewn across the tables in front of them, the floor sticky with booze. Eric Bristow was playing Dave Whitcombe in the semi-final.

Eric strode up to the oche, and the slurping, puffing hubbub subsided. Silence reigned. ('You could hear the drip off a chip.') Bristow in his blood-red Crafty Cockney shirt, mullet streaked with highlights, fag in hand, billowing smoke from his nostrils like a dragon, little finger delicately erect as he gripped his dart, as if sipping from the finest bone china, was dissecting Dave slowly and gloriously. His first dart hit the board with a deep, satisfying thud. Glen's and my saucer-wide eyes went from the distant board to a machine to one side of the stage where a rotund man with spreading sideburns, dressed in a maroon blazer, plugged a peg into a small socket and so lit up a display showing where the dart had landed. Treble 20. A murmur of approval spread among the darting cognoscenti around the hall. Bristow threw again. Another thud. Another treble 20. Another light lit in the red skinny bit. The murmur turned into gasps of anticipation. On TV, the camera would be zooming in on the treble 20 bed, but we didn't have that luxury here. It didn't matter. The noise, the crowd, the lights, the fug all made it far more exciting than on the telly. Another thud, another light lit. And then the crowd erupted: a guttural, intimidating, ear-splitting roar that drowned out even Freddie Williams' booming call of 'Un-undred-an-eyeteeeeeh!' Bristow raised his right hand in acknowledgement, took his darts from the board, turned and walked back to his mark, drawing deeply and triumphantly on his cig. Dave, who, in sharp contrast to his charismatic, strutting opponent, looked like a chubby trainspotter on a rare night out, mopped his sodden brow with a handkerchief. ('He's sweatin' like a puddin' in a pot.')

From there we were whisked around the back of the hall, through the beery miasma, to a tiny prefab wooden box. An enormous man in another maroon blazer – paired with some highly flammable-looking blue trousers, which were the uniform of the British Darts Organisation (BDO) – stood at the foot of a small set of portable steps, which led to its door. He held up a huge hairy hand.

Me, Robbie and our granddad on a baking afternoon on Dalton Avenue, Lynemouth.

Bob, Martha and a baby Derrick on the steps of their house in Ellington.

Bob (second from right) with his beloved Bedlington terrier, Swank.

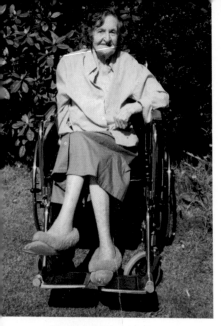

Martha in her last few weeks. She was still being wheeled out to smoke a tab or two until the end.

Sid in his graduation photo from Cambridge, with what appears to be a dead skunk on his back.

Below: Bob, Derrick, Martha, Sid and Derrick's best man on his wedding day. A picture of joy... save the wintry presence of Mary Jane to the far right.

Charles E. Hall and Sid – the Gravyboatmen (*photo courtesy of Charles E. Hall*).

Sid and Lindsey on their wedding day.

Sid and Lindsey toast their union with the best man and bridesmaid, Terry and Marge.

Top: Bob and Martha in a rare embrace. The photo on the right is taken outside their hotel room on their sole visit together to the darts.

Above: The *Calendar* team in 1972 for its 1,000th episode. Sid is in the centre, complete with Teddy boy haircut. To his direct left is Donald Baverstock, his voluble and unpredictable mentor.

Left: Sid and Eric Bristow after winning a pro-am tournament. Sid was a bad darts player and this was the only trophy he ever won.

Sid on *Celebrity It's a Knockout* in 1981. There weren't enough red noses to go round so his was painted on, and he could barely walk because of gout.

Sid and Tony Green in the commentary box.

Below: Irene, Sid, me and Dammsy dressed to kill for the darts at Lakeside in 1989 (*photo courtesy of Richard Damms*).

Above left: Among the ruins in Rhodes in 1985.

Above right: Sid and I catch the sun in Portugal in 1986.

Right: Swigging a lunchtime beer... aged 14.

Below: Sid in skimpy red shorts doing what he called 'sun worshipping'.

Above: Jocky Wilson's greatest fan. Here Sid is dressed up – complete with toilet roll sporran – for a darts lunch.

Above: Sid was never shy when it came to initiating a sing-song, and was hardly off the mic at the nightly cabarets which followed the darts.

Right: Sid's unique rules of commentary, written in his inimitable 'dead spider' scrawl.

Sid, me and a couple of punters ahead of the World Darts final in 1989 (*photo courtesy of Richard Damms*).

My sisters and me. Lucy, Charlotte and Emma.

Below: Sid was a hands-off dad but a devoted grandfather. Here he reads to my son Dougie.

'Sid's son and his mate,' said our guide.

The maroon giant put his hand down and grinned. My chest swelled fit to burst. Being Sid's son had gained me few favours elsewhere, but it obviously did here. Our guide put his hand to his lips to encourage our silence, then led us up the stairs. On stage, Bristow hit a double to take the leg. Beyond the door, I could hear my dad's muffled banshee Geordie cry. The door flew open, and we were bundled in.

He was sat facing a monitor, cans on his ears, the band across the top overgrown by his mass of curly dark-brown hair, a microphone pressed to his mouth. He saw us, put down the mic and gave us a manic two-handed wave. Then he pointed exaggeratedly at two chairs directly behind his seat. We sat down. He turned back to his monitor, picked up the mic and returned to his performance. My first impression was of how small the box was. My dad wasn't a big man, but his energy was uncontainable. In a room so tiny, he was 'like a buffalo in an airing cupboard' (that was Dylan Thomas not Sid Waddell, but it could have been one of his).

The window in front faced the stage, but none of the three men in the box were looking out of it. The air within was just as thick with smoke as without. Tony Green, my dad's co-commentator, was to our far right in the 'spotter's' chair. It was his job to tell the producer sitting in the scanner in the car park, directly alongside the club's dustbins, which way the players might finish, which trebles and doubles they would aim for, so he could instruct the cameramen and no shot would be missed. He did this while working his way through a string of gratis cigarettes provided by the sponsor, Embassy. He stubbed one out and lit up another. Beside him was Harry Coventry, whose job it was to log the scores and keep my dad and Tony fed with stats with which to punctuate their commentary: how many 180s, highest checkouts, that sort of thing. Harry turned and smiled, while Tony nodded a greeting, his face wreathed by a blue haze of smoke. On stage, Bristow hit double 16, his favourite, to take the set.

'With all the accuracy of a Kalashnikov rifle,' my dad screamed.

I looked at Glen and we giggled. My dad had never fired a gun in his life. But that wasn't why we laughed. Until then he'd been subdued, whispering, restrained. But now he was on his feet shouting and lunging towards his screen like a centre forward stretching for a header. I was half-mortified, half-entranced. That double had put Bristow in an unassailable position.

'The rug was pulled and the mat was sent!' Dad shouted and sat back down.

I didn't understand that line. But it didn't matter. It sounded good, and we still giggled. It's stuck with me ever since, and I now know what he meant. The mangling and mixing of cliché to create a vivid image was one of my dad's favourite tropes. 'The rug was pulled' of course alludes to the cliché of pulling the rug from under someone's feet, as Brissy was no doubt doing to Dave; 'and the mat was sent' is a reference to someone being 'on the mat', like a spent wrestler, whom Dave resembled and at 5–1 down definitely was. Yoking the two together conjures up an inspired image of a toppling Dave hitting the canvas, even if my twelve-year-old self just thought it was my dad being daft again. (I have a friend who once sat in the commentary box with me and who to this day is still baffled by

my dad's description of Bristow as 'a pterodactyl in winter' . . .
I did ask my dad about that one. His answer was long, but in a
nutshell: 'Bristow was going through an unsuccessful period in
his career, waiting for the form to return that would allow him
to reclaim his rightful throne. It brought to mind Shakespeare's
description of Richard III as a "Lion in Winter", except that
Eric with his beaked nose and piercing stare was more pterodactyl than lion . . .')

He put the mic down, switched it to talkback, and turned to
Glen and me. He winked at us both.

'Good 'ere, innit?'

It was, Glen and I agreed. The game ended, my dad gathered
the pile of papers, used envelopes and other scraps on which
he'd scribbled his notes and stuffed them in his bag. Then he
burst out of the door and we followed. My father walked quicker
than any man I've ever met, and here, the nervous energy that
fuelled his performance still coursing through him, he was out
of the traps like a greyhound. Glen and I struggled to keep up.
But there was another reason for him to walk so fast. As he
made his way around the back of the audience, a few of the fans
saw him.

'Sid!'

'Why aye, kidda!'

'The greatest comeback since Lazarus!'

'Jocky on the oche!'

The shouts, his name, lines he'd said in commentary, all
came thick and fast. A beery, glassy-eyed throng was soon
trying to envelop him. He did his best to smile and sign a few
autographs, while making sure Glen and I didn't get swallowed
by the huddled, befuddled masses. But it took fifteen minutes

to make a thirty-second journey. I couldn't believe he was this well liked and appreciated.

My dad, famous?

It seemed absurd.

Jossy's Giants

IN 1982, AFTER a couple of years scoring prolifically as a centre forward at primary school, I joined a newly formed club team in Leeds with a couple of friends. Churwell was a small village on the slope of a hill on the other side of Leeds to Pudsey, the birthplace of former prime minister Herbert Asquith and industrial philanthropist Titus Salt. But that wasn't the attraction. They needed players, which meant we would get a game, and their coach had been a former professional.

Up to a point. Walter 'Sonny' Sweeney was the captain of Scotland under-15s and was lured south to play for Don Revie's Leeds United in 1964. He came down at the same time as Eddie Gray. But alas, whereas Eddie established himself in Revie's first great Leeds side, Sonny only managed a few matches before heading back to Scotland to play for Greenock Morton and then on to Ireland to play for Cork Hibernians. However, Sonny had met his wife in Leeds and moved back there in the 1970s.

In between working as a salesman, he did some coaching for his old Leeds teammate Bobby Collins at his academy as well as acting as a Northern scout for Ipswich Town. Eventually, he had time to set up Churwell Lions in 1982, and I was among the first intake. We had some decent players and some good results, but pitched into a league against more cohesive, seasoned teams we also suffered some hideous hammerings. 'These Lions don't roar,' as Sid was often fond of saying.

Matches were Sunday mornings. As Sid didn't drive, we always cadged a lift. Unlike when he watched me play cricket, where he would remain quiet, nursing a pint, he was far more vocal on the sidelines at football, often embarrassingly so. But he was never as loud as Sonny. 'Skun 'um!' he would shout at our winger. 'Jockey! Jockey!' he would cry, urging the defence to stay on their feet and usher the attacker to the wing rather than dive in to the tackle. He lived every agonizing second of our matches, and agony was commonplace, emotionally and physically. But his enthusiasm never relented; it was as if he was working out the thwarted ambition of his stunted professional career.

His team talks, delivered in a thick Scottish brogue, were legendary. He had a tactics board, in reality a small fold-up cardboard football pitch, on which he would move Subbuteo figures. A few went missing, so he filled in with a Father Christmas from a Christmas cake and some Star Wars figures. Yoda and Santa as part of a magical midfield four. Yet we still lost.

He was an innovator too. After one match in a blizzard on top of a moor, where we ended the match with only seven players as frozen kids trooped off in tears to avoid exposure, he gave us all bin bags with armholes cut in them to wear underneath our kit. It worked, but for the opposition the jokes wrote themselves. One stout opposition centre back christened us all 'Russell' because of the incessant noise. There was also a cutting, colourful line of criticism when his frustration at our short-comings overcame him. 'Too many prima donnas and not enough Maradonas,' he once said. Or was that my dad?

This was territory too fertile for Sid to ignore. By the end of my first season, he had started developing the idea that would become *Jossy's Giants*, transposing a Geordie ex-pro for a Glaswegian. He mined the Lions and their parents and their personalities for more ideas, and soon he had a finished script, which was commissioned by the BBC in mid 1985.

Filming began in the winter of 1985–86. By this time I had left the Lions to play for a newly founded team that continued the fierce cat/crap team theme, Pudsey Panthers. But I and a few select Panthers were invited to join the Lions for a day of filming. We would make up the opposition facing the eponymous Giants, who subject them to a humiliating defeat and arouse the sympathy of a passing Jossy.

We were asked to play with swagger and arrogance, which came naturally to none of us. It was also an education in the tedious reality of filming. The director explained he needed a wide shot for the opening shot of the series, which was to be of the Giants ground with a game going on in the background. He would then cut to a series of shots of us attacking and scoring against the hapless home team.

He called action, and we started. The ball was swept down the left to me, I ran up the wing, the first signs of an eighties mullet bobbing on the back of my neck (method acting), before crossing into the middle, where my fellow Panther Simon Briggs swept an immaculate volley into the top corner, cueing tumultuous, genuine celebration from all concerned. That would look *fantastic* on television.

Except that was only the wide shot. The cameras were moved to take closer shots of the cross and the shot. We needed to do it again. But next time my cross wasn't so pinpoint. And when it was, Briggsy's shooting was terrible. After ten takes, with everyone having a go, no one had scored a goal. We had shot wide, over or fluffed it completely. Eventually, someone managed to score and put us and the crew out of our misery. An hour's filming had taken four. A fight nearly erupted when one cast member was heard to remark to another that he could see where the writer had got his inspiration for making the Giants so crap.

The show was screened in 1986 and attracted six million viewers. An equally popular second series followed the year after, and nearly thirty years on the series is remembered with great fondness by a certain generation, for its terrible cameo by Bryan Robson, who took to acting like he did football management, but mainly for its distinctive theme tune. Doing his best Dennis Waterman impression, Sid did try to write the theme tune, to the air of a Geordie folk song, 'Wor Geordie's Lost 'Is Penka', about a young man's attempt to find his lost marble. Thankfully, his effort was overlooked in favour of a much catchier, distinctive one written by Mike Amatt. Ask anyone what they remember of the series and inevitably they'll nod their head twice and go, 'Duh duh Jossy's Giants!'

On the back of its success, Sid tried to use my experience as a cricketer to write an adult comedy about a cricket club. I remember reading page one, scene one:

EXT day. A woman is shown instructing her son in the virtues of a long stride in a forward defensive:
'Leg over, leg over . . . Get your leg over!'

Cut to her husband walking past the hedge, the woman and boy unseen.

'Chance'd be a fine thing,' he mutters.

For everyone's benefit, not least Sid's future career, the 'adult' comedy was excised and the show recast as *Jossy's Giants* but about cricket. *Sloggers*, as it was known, also ran for two series on children's BBC, though I think Sid agreed it was not as good as *Jossy*. It did launch Ralf Little's career, he would claim proudly, though I'm not sure anyone who endured *Two Pints of Lager and a Packet of Crisps* would thank him for it.

Future World Champions

I DON'T REMEMBER SEEING much of Sid when I was a young boy. Both he and Irene worked hard; Sid left in the morning before I woke up and arrived back late in the evening either just before or after I went to bed. He was around at weekends, but I don't remember doing anything with him other than him watching me play cricket in the summer and football in the winter. And often his work for the children's TV department meant he had to work on Saturdays, because Manchester were given the rights to produce the summer equivalent of *Noel Edmonds' Swap Shop* (programmes like *Get Set for Summer*, *The 8.15 from Manchester*, and other unlamented shows). Though Charlotte, Emma and I would occasionally travel over to be part of the audience.

So the chance in 1985 to spend a weekend with him at the darts was too good to miss. The morning after our night at the semi-finals, Glen and I were up early, despite having spent most of the night enjoying the novelty of a TV in our room. Irene was not getting up to take us to breakfast, so that was left to Sid. The only complication was that he was hungover; he may even have still been pissed. The morning after, Sid was always tightly wound and sensitive. I still have traumatic memories of a train journey back to Leeds from London with him the day after he had been on the booze. Every other word was 'fuck'. At one stage, I went to the buffet car and stood there with my coffee until we were nearer home, because without me there I thought he might fall asleep. Eventually, I returned to my seat. 'Where the fuck have you been?' he snarled.

That morning he was twitchy. I sat down while Glen, who had never stayed in a hotel and had a hearty appetite, drifted around the buffet as if in a reverie.

With two working parents, I was a self-sufficient kid used to feeding, clothing and bathing myself. But Sid wasn't around enough to know that. I sat sipping orange juice while he asked me a million questions. 'Do you want some cereal? Do you want some toast? Do you want a glass of milk?' He kept racing back from the buffet with food I'd not even asked for, creating such a fuss that people turned to watch. I sank lower in my seat, wanting the flock carpet to swallow me whole. Yes, I had discovered that my dad was famous, and that was cool, but he could also be very embarrassing in public. (In my teenage years, when I was mortified by anything remotely uncomfortable, Sid would deliberately turn the embarrassment dial up to 11 to amuse himself.)

'I got you some Weetabix. Here.' The biscuits were in individual packets. He started ripping them open so cack-handedly that shards of wheat flew everywhere. 'Fuck!' he hissed.

An Australian voice boomed across the room.

'Strewth, Sid, give the kid a break. You gonna wipe his arse next?'

It was Terry O'Dea, Australia's finest player, one of my heroes and built like a brick dunny. Sid was speechless. I felt bad for him but also glad because it meant he would leave me alone. Through the Weetabix shower, I'd watched Glen pile his plate high with bacon, sausage, eggs – the full lot. I wanted a cooked breakfast, not boring cereal.

'Can I go get some bacon and eggs, Dad?'

He nodded and winked at me, as if to say sorry. Just then Glen sat down, the leaning tower of breakfast threatening to landslide messily from his plate on to the table. Sid smiled, almost relaxed now he'd been told off, as if it was some sort of performance he'd needed to do and was glad to put behind him.

'Fill yer boots, kidda.'

~

All morning and all afternoon, Glen and I did nothing but throw darts. There were two boards in the hotel bar where the players had practised all week. Now most of them were knocked out, though none had gone home, they were free until night-time when the money matches began.

I don't think we stopped for two hours. Both of us were intoxicated with what we had witnessed the night before. I was a talented cricketer but all that could go hang: who wanted the acclaim of a suited crowd at Lord's when you could win the acclaim of a thousand men in cardigans at Stoke and a nation watching at home at teatime on Saturday, live on *Grandstand*?

We barely saw Sid for the rest of the day. He slept, drank water, gorged on sausage rolls and rested his voice in preparation for the Lowe–Bristow final everyone was convinced would be a classic. Glen and I threw darts. Then Tony Gubba and a BBC crew walked in with John Lowe, natty in a blue tank top. We carried on throwing, affecting nonchalance, expecting to be thrown out any minute when they started filming.

But the director asked us to carry on playing. They wanted to film Lowe's interview, some establishing shots of him sipping a cup of tea, and then throwing some practice darts with us in the background, all for *Grandstand*. Glen went up to the board to throw after this had been explained to us. His hand was shaking so much he couldn't release it. *Grandstand*?! Us?! Our lives centred on it. We'd have a kickabout on a Saturday morning, then back in time for fish and chips and *Football Focus*. Sometimes you'd be able to guess which grounds the *Match of the Day* cameras were at depending on where their reporters were. Then it'd be horse racing, which was Glen's love. We'd pick a horse and bet pennies. Then a bit of a wait until the rugby league and the scores flashing up. Sometimes Glen's dad would come back after a lunchtime session and play-fight with us, often going too far by sitting on us – he was nearly twenty stone. It ended with *Final Score*. That was our Saturday every week. But now we were to appear on it.

We didn't get to watch it. By the time it was screened, we were in the crowd at Jollees, passively smoking enough fags to last a lifetime but enthralled at the din as the crowd chanted 'John! Lowe!' and then 'Bristow!' back and forth. Back at home in Pudsey though, Glen's grandma was watching the build-up and saw us appear without warning. She was in her seventies, but she sprinted down the street to his mum's house to tell her, tears of joy rolling down her face. 'Our Glen is on the telly.' They could hear her screams in Armley jail.

Nobody recorded it. Neither of us got to watch it until a couple of years ago when it was uploaded to YouTube. There's Lowe sipping delicately from fine china, and there's twelve-year-old Glen and me throwing darts in terrible jumpers. Tony Gubba describes us as 'world champions of the future'. That didn't come to pass. It has a strange haunting quality, like watching a ghost of your own self, which I suppose it is. Jollees has gone, *Grandstand* too, as well as Glen's dear old gran, but our bad arrers and questionable knitwear have been preserved for the ages.

Bristow won the final convincingly. This was the start of his golden period, when he looked unbeatable, until the onset of the dreaded dartitis robbed him of his chance to dominate the decade completely. But for a few sets we revelled in the atmosphere and tumult; those around us seemed to live every dart. We weren't allowed back in the commentary box, but we enjoyed being part of the crowd even more. Even better, afterwards we went backstage, where we saw the players up close: Bristow triumphant, John Lowe disappointed but dignified in defeat. It seemed weird to see them supping lager and chatting with their mates only a few minutes after seeing them snarl and chuck on stage. We clutched our programmes and asked as many players that were sober enough to scribble their names. Then, one by one, people left, the set came down, and Jollees was transformed from a stage of great sporting drama back to a cheap cabaret club. Irene and Sid had gone to the post-tournament dinner, so Glen and I threw more darts on the practice boards behind the stage, but they had to come down too. We stood and watched as all evidence of the World Championship was packed away for another year. It had a horrible Sunday night, after-the-carnival-is-over feeling.

That night as we drove away through the rain-soaked streets of Stoke back to Yorkshire, a spent and exhausted Sid dozing in the passenger seat up front, I felt empty: as if life would only ever seem ordinary after experiencing such extraordinary thrills. I promised myself to never miss a World Championship again.

I fulfilled that vow for the next twelve years.

Deep Heat

T HE FIRST THING I heard was a sickening squelch, like the sound of a chicken's neck being wrung. But it was my neck. I'd turned over in bed, half asleep, or rather my neck had. My body had not followed, and something had been strained or pulled. The sear of pain that followed felt like I had been branded. I had cricked my neck, which wouldn't have been so bad, but the next day I was supposed to be playing cricket for Yorkshire under-15s against our rivals Lancashire. The North of England selectors would be there, and I had an outside chance of making the team for the England Schools Cricket Festival in London in August.

Head kinked at an odd angle, I walked into my dad's bedroom.

'I've hurt my neck,' I said dolefully.

Downstairs, Sid gave me a quick examination. 'I divven't think it's that bad, kidda,' he pronounced. I would have been reassured had Sid a) known the first thing about physiotherapy and b) not been the sort of person who always says what some-one else wants to hear.

I also think it's what he wanted to believe. Not because he

was a pushy dad. He was the opposite. A number of my team-mates were afflicted with fathers who had been good cricketers and were desperate for their sons to do well. If they played a poor shot, or bowled badly, or dropped a catch, their fathers were on to them, chastising and criticizing. I saw the passion die in the eyes of a number of talented boys who lost interest because their dads piled pressure on them, draining all the fun from the game.

Not for me. Sid knew as much about cricket as he did about clay pigeon shooting (though that didn't stop him commentating on clay pigeon shooting in later life, but that's another story). I'd be out for a duck, and whereas most kids would avoid the parental eye, Sid was there with a clap on the back. 'Never mind, kidda,' he'd say and stand me a Fanta and a bag of ready salted Seabrooks. I piled on weight during a bad run of form.

Two summers before, I'd been playing for Pudsey St Lawrence's third team at Farsley Celtic. We were a man short, so Sid was drafted in. He was a bag of nerves, had a coughing fit and ten minutes before the start of the game heaved mightily behind the scorebox. It got more embarrassing from there.

He dropped two catches. When he went out to bat, he was called for a quick single. He was run out by half the length of the pitch because his box had slipped out of the side of his baggy Y-fronts and fallen out of the bottom of his trouser leg, and he stooped to pick it up.

But as my cricket improved, and I started to be picked for regional and representative teams, my dad's desire to see me do well grew. He knew the importance of the match against Lancashire, who in John Crawley and Ronnie Irani boasted two England players of the future. My cricked neck wasn't going to spoil my chances of playing.

'It needs some heat,' he said. I thought he meant Deep Heat, which was his cure-all for everything, along with Andrews Liver Salts. Something told me that wouldn't work.

'Nah, I mean real heat.'

Later that morning, he returned with a sun lamp. It was covered in dust, forgotten and stored in someone's attic for years.

'Sit down,' he said. He turned on the lamp and tilted it at my neck. 'That should do it.'

The next morning, when I woke up, the first thing I did was try to move my neck. There was much more movement and much less pain. But then I touched it . . .

I walked into Irene and Sid's bedroom. 'The good news is that I can move my neck. The bad news is that I have sunburn.'

The whole side of my face and neck was red raw. It turned out I had minor sunstroke.

I still played. I scored 98 but was unable to field because of vomiting and nausea. But I was selected to represent the North of England. Sid had enjoyed a few beers in the bar during the match and was ebullient after.

'I knew the heat'd work a trick,' he said.

Lakeside

O N SID AND Irene's voluminous bookshelves was a little-read tome. It was called *The Story of Lakeside*, a lavishly illustrated, privately printed history of the club as told by its owner, Bob Potter. It recounted how Bob, a self-made man and proud of it, had a dream of owning the finest cabaret club in the land. In 1972, he built the first incarnation, which sadly and tragically burned down in 1978. There were photos of Bob looking mournful among the smoking ruins. But like a phoenix from the ashes, a cliché the book was not afraid to use liberally, a new, better Lakeside arose. All the stars played there: Jim Davidson, Tom Jones, Shirley Bassey and Roger De Courcey with Nookie the Bear.

The British Darts Organisation now tout Lakeside as the home of British darts. But such an accolade seemed unlikely in 1986 when the World Championship moved there. First of all, it was not just in the south but in Camberley, a depressing embodiment of dreary middle England and the Home Counties: mock-Tudor mansions in gated communities, ye olde pubbes, and populated by the nouveaux riches. Miles away from earthy, smoky Stoke and its working-class community. Unlike Jollees, with its sticky, sloping floors, Formica tables and pie and chips, Lakeside was all carpets (emblazoned with the Lakeside logo, naturally), fake chandeliers and chicken in a basket. Jollees unapologetically styled itself as a brassy night out; the Lakeside featured many of the same acts but sought to add a layer of sophistication, with two 'f's.

But I loved every tacky bit of it. If the darts ever bored us, we'd go to the gallery that featured portraits of all the acts who had appeared there. Among established names such as the Nolan Sisters, Cliff Richard, Jimmy Cricket and the Grumbleweeds were lesser-known performers like the Maori Volcanic Showband and risqué dance act Rampage.

While the atmosphere never matched the smoggy hysteria of Jollees, it achieved a unique one of its own. It was glitzier, smarter and lot more comfortable for paying punters. And unlike in Jollees, you could see the darts from nearly any part of the auditorium.

∼

That first year in 1986, Glen and I and another mate, Simon, were driven down to Lakeside by Simon's dad on the Friday morning at dawn. There we would meet my stepbrother Nick and his mate Mr Silly, who had travelled via London and all pubs in between. Sid met us at the hotel, the Ladbroke Mercury in Bracknell; Bob Potter's on-site hotel was still then but a dream. As ever, we didn't have tickets but passes. That meant we didn't have seats but we could access all areas, allowing us to soak up the unique ambience backstage. As these were reserved for the families of officials, Sid hit upon a wheeze he would use for championships thereafter: we all had the surname Waddell. There was me and Nick (surname actually Cockroft) who were legitimately family, then came Glen Waddell, Simon Waddell, his dad Stuart Waddell, and Nick's mate Dave Waddell. No one batted an eyelid or seemed surprised that Sid had fathered so many children by at least five different mothers.

Bristow had been cruising all week and dealt handily with Alan Glazier, the Man in Black, in the first semi. Glazier then gave me, Glen and Simon a lesson in darts backstage – teaching us stance, balance, sureness of throw – which I don't think was common behaviour among defeated semi-finalists in any sport. If that wasn't exciting enough, there were celebrities present backstage: John Virgo and Duncan Norvelle (nowadays Prince Harry is a regular, but royalty were few and far between in the 1980s).

We watched in awe as Bob Anderson warmed up for his match against Dave Whitcombe in a tasselled western shirt with his nickname 'The Limestone Cowboy' emblazoned on the back. This had been given to him by Sid because he lived in Derbyshire, the limestone county, though he was born in Hampshire. Bob had the good sense to run with it, perhaps sensing the way darts was heading and inspired by Eric's success as the Crafty Cockney. Compared to worthy but boring Whitcombe, we all decided to root for him. He lost a thriller 5–4.

Back at the hotel, Simon, Glen and I threw darts all night and kept a low profile to avoid being sent to bed. We were soon kicked off the boards by darters playing for cash, so we hid to the side of the hotel bar, sipping Coke furtively. Nick and Mr Silly were at the bar, smashed off their faces. The TV was turned on to show the highlights of that night's matches, and Sid slid off to hear how his commentary sounded. Dave Whitcombe approached the bar while in the background the screen showed him engaged in a ceaseless tussle with Anderson.

'Hang on, there's a bloke on the telly who looks exactly like you!' said Mr Silly.

'Nah,' said Whitcombe earnestly, as if Silly was stupid. 'It is me.'

Mr Silly is dead now. But somewhere he's still laughing about that.

Eventually we were sent up to bed, where we worked out how to watch porn. We were still watching it when the hotel fire alarm went off, and we had to traipse outside. Whitcombe was there drinking a pint of milk; Silly and Nick were still on the hard stuff.

The final was a non-event. Bristow won 6–0 and barely broke sweat. Sid was devastated because he had started the final but had not got back in to call the winning shot. He and Tony Green were friendly enough, but Sid had started to become paranoid that his partner was trying to sew up the best games by using his greater political nous and contacts in the darts world. This unease had been brewing for some time. Meanwhile, all the press attention he had been getting for his one-liners and excitable commentary was causing some resentment. Nearly every review of the darts mentioned Sid, and nearly every feature writer who travelled to Camberley sought him out for a quote – and oddly enough there were more correspondents and colour men who were willing to catch the short hop from Waterloo than were keen to make the long trip from Euston to Stoke. The result was that by the end of the week Sid was increasingly on edge and happy to have people around with whom he could relax.

He certainly relaxed that evening. He and Stuart stayed behind to attend the post-tournament dinner, while Nick and Mr Silly headed off in search of beer. Sid had organized for Glen, Simon and me to go back to the hotel on the shuttle bus that ran between Bracknell and Lakeside. The weather outside was icy cold, so we waited by the stage door with some of the players and crimplene-clad officials. The minibus pulled up, we all got on, and the driver disappeared inside, presumably to have a pee or look for stragglers. We waited and waited. The door opened and out staggered one incredibly pissed darts player who will remain nameless. He could barely walk.

The next thing we knew, he was in the driver's seat. Everyone started laughing. Very funny, they cried. They were soon screaming. The driver had left the keys in the ignition. The darts player started the engine, and we set off across the icy car park at high speed. The colour had drained completely from the face of the woman next to me. 'Stop him, stop him!' she screamed in genuine terror. Everyone was wailing and screeching. The van left the venue and headed straight across a roundabout. I'd given up – that was it, we were going to die. I closed my eyes and braced for impact. But another darts player had climbed into the front and managed to wrestle control and pull the van over. I'm sure he was also pissed, but he was at least able to see. He drove the van back to Bracknell as the other player snoozed beside him and the colour returned to our faces. Back in the hotel bar, we threw darts while our fellow passengers downed stiff drinks to recover their nerves, muttering darkly about having the offending player banned. But this was darts, and no one was ostracized for long. As we went to bed, our errant driver was leading the sing-song, forgiven.

Sid and Stuart had staggered in, both well gone. 'Get back all right?' Sid asked. I thought of telling him but decided against it. What if he thought twice about bringing us or letting us out of his sight? I loved the freedom we were given at the darts. I nodded.

'Good,' he said. 'Now get to bed.'

That night, we watched more blue movies. The next morning, Sid came to our room after breakfast. I could tell he was angry.

'Have you bastards been watching dirty films?'

We hung our heads. Best admit it and take the rap. 'A couple,' I said.

'A couple? *Lusty Au Pair Girls* one AND two, *The Pleasure Chamber*, *Schoolgirl Sluts*.' Glen started to snigger. Sid carried on, '*Swedish Massage Dream* . . . You watched them all!'

'Sorry, Dad.'

Sid looked apoplectic. Normally, his anger would pass as quickly as it arrived, far preferable to the slow-burn bollockings and withering put-downs that Irene handed out. But he was incandescent, more furious than he had ever been with me.

'How the hell am I gonna get these past expenses?'

The BBC were picking up the tab. Usually, they were generous, but there had recently been a scandal when the police were called after a couple of staffers had ordered hundreds of pounds' worth of booze and put it on the room of a less bibulous colleague. Sid would face some awkward questions, and that's why he was so upset. The pollution of our innocent minds was the least of his worries.

Maybe it was Glen sniggering, maybe it was our dopey faces, or wondering what the plot of *Swedish Massage Dream* was all about, but he soon started to laugh. 'It'll be a damn sight cheaper for me when you buggers get pissed and bring Embassy lasses back to your rooms.'

We were thirteen.

Fish Curry

M Y STEPBROTHER NICK returned from university with a head full of ideas and tubs of exotic Indian spices. One morning, he asked Sid and me if we fancied a curry. As I was not yet of drinking age, when most young Northern men started to eat curry, and Sid was more of a Chinese than an Indian man, we were both curious and agreed.

Later that afternoon, Sid and I were sitting in the back room in Pudsey when strange smells started to waft down the hall.

'This is gonna be interesting, kidda,' he said to me, as if we were guinea pigs for some strange medical procedure.

A few minutes later, he went to the kitchen. When he came back, his face wore the look of someone who had witnessed a loved one hacking a dead body to bits and stuffing it in a suitcase. He closed the door behind him. It was a sunny day, and the French windows to the garden had been thrown open. He walked over and closed them quietly. I watched, bemused. He turned to me, wide-eyed.

'He's making fish curry!' he hissed.

I pulled a 'hmm that's interesting' face.

'Fish!' he said. 'Have you ever had fish curry?'

I'd had curry about three times. Each involved chicken. 'No.'

He shook his head and pulled a face. 'Never even bloody heard of fish curry,' he mumbled.

For the next few hours, as the smells grew more pungent, Sid repeated the pattern. He'd get up, go to the kitchen, ostensibly to get a cup of coffee or a snack but really to spy on what Nick was doing. He'd return with more news, all of it shocking to him.

'Ooooh, he's putting onions in now!'

'He's using bloody ginger!'

'Aaaw, kid, you gotta see how much garlic the bugger is putting in!'

'I divven't knaa what them spices are, but he's hoying them in there by the spoonful!'

'He's put a chilli in it and he never even chopped the bastard! Just lobbed it straight in.'

And the recurring one: 'Have you ever heard of bloody fish in a curry?'

Occasionally, he would double over and grab his belly in theatrical fashion.

Finally, the curry was ready. Nick called us in and we walked down the hall, Sid like a condemned man on his way to the gallows. 'I'm not sure whether to say Grace or the Last fucking Rites!' he muttered.

We sat down. The curry was light brown; onions, flakes of cod and some vegetables were bobbing appetizingly near the surface. A bowl of perfectly cooked rice billowed clouds of steam in the middle of the table. It looked and smelled gorgeous.

As we took our seats, Nick was still coming in and out of the kitchen with food and bowls.

'Looks great, kidda,' my dad said.

Nick went back to the kitchen; Sid looked across at me, raised his eyebrows and made the sign of the cross.

Nick joined us and we tucked in. It tasted delicious.

'Bloody hell, that's actually nice!' Sid said, unable to contain his surprise.

There was a silence as we ate appreciatively. It had a kick to it, and every now and then Sid would shake his head and go, 'Whoah! Good for me catarrh this, son,' then sniff theatrically.

'What's them green things?'

'Green beans,' Nick told him.

Sid grimaced as if it was a monkey's finger but ploughed on to the end. 'That were dead good,' he said as he finished his plate and mopped his brow.

～

Sid was no foodie. All the foods he enjoyed as a kid – pies, pasties, soups, baked beans and cups of hot Bovril with Jacob's Cream Crackers broken up and mixed in – he ate as a man. He preferred tinned peas to frozen; instant coffee to freshly ground; Marmite to marmalade; jars of pasta sauce to a slow-cooked ragu; and sliced bread to ciabatta. He balked at any hint of pretension. 'I've never eaten yoghurt in me life,' he once said to me proudly, as if yoghurt was the embodiment of the bourgeoisie and not a staple in the diets of some of the world's most impoverished nations. The look he gave me when I told him I once added full-fat milk to a bolognese sauce told you all you need to know about his view of TV chefs and their recipes.

And yet . . . success did bring with it a few trappings. His gout and general allergic reaction to red wine meant he developed a taste for Pinot Grigio and Chardonnay, poured in huge measures that appalled my oenophile brother-in-law. (I once used the word oenophile to my dad: 'Any bugger who uses the word oenophile is an onanist,' he said. 'It's just a posh term for piss artist.') Olives were another guilty pleasure. I only saw him eat them at home. The same with balsamic vinegar on salad, but I think he saw that as posh Worcestershire sauce.

So it was no surprise that he was not a fan of fine dining. His favourite restaurants were backstreet Italians with gingham tablecloths and Chianti served in baskets. La Perla on Brewer Street was a port of call whenever he was in London, complete with a glass of grappa, each sip accompanied by a theatrical wince. Another staple was a place opposite King's Cross whose name escapes me, where it was more about the ambience – or the 'ambulance' as he called it. Garlic prawns, spaghetti vongole and some cheap plonk and he was happy as a pig in parsley.

Much of his later life was spent on the road, eating in hotels, wolfing down pasties, queuing to be fed from the Sky chuck wagon at the venue. I asked him what he did for breakfast when he was away for a week at a time in hotels. Did he skip it? Eat muesli? 'Never,' he said. He explained his routine: 'First morning and last morning full English. Alternate sausage sandwich and bacon sandwich each day in between.'

The first thing he did when he got home was have pie and peas and some Bovril. It's a wonder he lived as long as he did.

Edge of Darkness

THE MID TO late 1980s were Sid's commentary salad days. Greater performances might come in the Sky era, but his commentaries for the BBC after the 'Deller Final' got better and better, drawing attention from wider afield than sport. The great *Guardian* TV critic Nancy Banks-Smith said of him in 1984: 'Sid Waddell's commentaries are the black pudding of sports reporting, hot and bursting with blood and guts.'

This was the era of many of his famous lines: 'Bristow reasons; Bristow quickens: aaaah, Bristow'; 'Cliff [Lazarenko]'s idea of exercise is a firm press on the soda siphon'; 'Kenny [Summers] proves that not all darts players are philistines: he runs a bookshop in Peterborough'; 'Jocky is sweating like a swamp donkey'; 'Jocky Wilson . . . what an athlete', and many others.

His confidence was growing. Gone were the prepared one-liners, though one he did crowbar in became his most famous, at the start of the 1984 final between Whitcombe and Bristow: 'Alexander of Macedonia had conquered the known world by the time he was thirty-three. Bristow's only twenty-six.' With typical Sid embellishment, over the years this has been gilded with the observation that Sid said Alexander 'cried salt tears', a wonderful adornment (though salt as opposed to what other tears?) but not one he said. But the original has bathos and power to spare as it is.

Rather than spend time preparing lines, he focused more intensively on researching players. Until the end of his career, he would pore obsessively over his notes and profiles of each player, compiled in his spidery scrawl. Only when this work was done, and he was confident that there was no more he could learn, was he able to enter the commentary box in a good frame of mind. Then he was able to relax and let the one-liners flow.

His knowledge and recall of books he had read was encyclopaedic. His favourite book was *Henderson the Rain King* by Saul Bellow, which he read in his teens several times. I read it when I was seventeen, and three weeks later he was able to remember much more of it than me. He could even recite chunks of the text.

He read widely and broadly. In the same way he believed darts to be the equal of other sports, he did not believe in literary distinctions. He was equally at ease discussing the pristine sentences of Booker winner John Banville as he was the biography of a Premier League footballer. Snippets of both would inform his commentary.

He revelled in language, high and low. The etymology of words fascinated him, as did slang terms and dialect. Another favourite novel was James Kelman's *How Late It Was, How Late*, the story of a Glasgow drunk, written entirely in stream-of-consciousness Scottish dialect. I found it unreadable; Sid relished it. When it won the Booker Prize, I pointed out that

Rabbi Julia Neuberger had called it 'crap' and stormed off the panel when it won; meanwhile, Simon Jenkins of *The Times* described it as literary vandalism. 'Snobs,' was Sid's verdict. 'They wanna deny the working class a voice.'

That probably makes Sid sound like a revolutionary. He was actually apolitical: a 'lager socialist', in that his views grew more left-wing according to how much he'd drunk. Sober he was known to vote Liberal Democrat; drunk and he was a Jimmy Reid-quoting class warrior. More often than not, Irene voted alone. When, at the 2010 election, Pudsey returned a Tory MP, Sid exploded with fury. Irene calmly reminded him that he hadn't bothered to vote and it had happened because of lazy buggers like him.

More important for his commentaries than his erudition was the sharpness of his mind, which allowed him to process a thought or a joke and verbalize it almost instantly, while the minds of the rest of us were still whirring. At one tiresome party of TV folk, a group had started to play charades: not really Sid's thing. 'Too many posers,' a word he often used for those who took themselves too seriously and believed themselves to be intellectual. One man mimed a TV show, held up three fingers to indicate how many words, then stepped backwards, hitting a table and almost knocking over a lamp.

'*Edge of Darkness*,' said Sid.

As he gained the confidence to extemporize in his commentary, the one-liners flowed and so too did viewers' appreciation, though there was always the obligatory complaint in *Darts World*. 'I wish to voice complaint as to the television commentary of Sid Waddell,' wrote Allen F. O'Reilly of Epsom, Surrey. 'The excellent presentation of the BBC was killed dead by his inane yammer.' His harshest critics were often diehard darts fans who wanted statistics – how many darts per leg, averages and checkout percentages – rather than references to the works of Robert Louis Stevenson or the lyrics of Fats Domino.

When he joined Sky, his freedom was unconfined. 'You don't produce Sid,' said his producer Rory Hopkins once. 'You let him out of the cage.' But the strict rules of the BBC, and the watchful eye of Nick Hunter, who wanted Sid's flair but allied to some discipline, did restrain him. Between those shackles and Sid's desire to innovate and entertain, as well as his innate insecurity and paranoia, there was a creative tension that informed the best commentaries of the period.

But at the heart of it were the players. Ordinary men with an extraordinary talent whose virtues Sid never tired of extolling. There were few airs and graces or pretensions among them: 'No posers here,' as Sid would say. Just men capable of great darts, in a sport spewing molten drama. Sid saw his role not as the Messiah but as the messenger. 'I'm not Jesus,' he said once, with typical modesty. 'I'm Moses.'

By now he was a cult figure. ('How you spelling that?' he'd always ask when it was mentioned.) He appeared on *It's A Celebrity Knockout* in 1981 in Blackpool with chronic gout. To the horror of us in the crowd, there were not enough clown costumes to go round the assembled celebrities, so Sid skipped and limped around at the start in shorts, T-shirt and a red nose. He was a regular in the 'Colemanballs' section of *Private Eye* ('He's been burning the midnight oil at both ends'; 'The fans with their eyes pierced to the dartboard') until the editor suspected he was coming up with such statements solely to be included (he might have had a point . . .), and he was thereafter banned.

It brought other gigs. My cricket club asked him to commentate on a charity day whose highlight was a competition to guess where a donkey had a crap. The donkey didn't arrive, so someone found a horse. The pitch was divided into many squares, people paid for one, and if the horse took a dump in their square they won. Sid sat freezing cold on a gantry above the clubhouse and tried to do his best to make this enthralling, fuelled by many pints of Webster's Bitter. If only the horse had been supplied with some cleansing Yorkshire ale. It was constipated and took hours to shit, by which time everyone was inside.

Despite the growing acclaim, the darts earned him little money, though it opened up other avenues. He compiled two books about darts for the BBC, he ghosted autobiographies of John Lowe and Jocky Wilson, and wrote a whimsical account of the game, *Bedside Darts*. None of them troubled the bestseller lists. I accompanied him on his one and only signing of *Bedside Darts*, at Menzies in Newcastle, en route to Lynemouth. His publishers expected the locals to flock to see their local boy made good. In an hour, one person bought a copy and admitted to Sid it was because he felt sorry for him.

There was no danger of him giving up the day job.

Fatter Belly

THE DARTS SOON became the highlight of my year. Forget Christmas: the only fat man in red I waited all year to see was Olly Croft. It became a chance to share some precious time with my dad too, which wasn't available to my sisters, who were less enamoured with the beery, sweaty throng at a darts match. As I had learned, anything went at the darts: I could stay up late, watch blue movies, even have a Jacuzzi, though sharing that with three darts players wasn't always a pleasant experience. The darts meant freedom and Sid.

Minus Glen, Simon and I returned to Lakeside in 1987, where I remember Jocky Wilson getting annihilated in the semi-finals by John Lowe and being so drunk afterwards that he got Sid in a headlock while repeatedly telling him that he loved him. 'I love you too, Jocky,' Sid repeated while being strangled. 'Now please let me go.' Eventually he did. 'Thank God he didn't win,' said Sid, rubbing his bruised neck.

Jocky appeared, even to my naive teenage eyes, well refreshed on stage that evening. Or, as Sid used to say, 'guilty of over-preparation' or 'over-psyched'. He had to employ such euphemisms over the years when he knew a player was drunk, given the omerta surrounding alcohol and darts, a consequence of David Vine's comments in 1978 and the Fatter Belly sketch. It always surprised me how sensitive those around the sport were when drink was raised. I remember one prominent BDO official being furious at a BBC montage which showed a clearly paralytic man in the crowd slump over and send a table of drinks flying. 'Terrible! The bastards!' he hissed. Even though that bloke was one of the most sober there.

If a football commentator learned a player was starting a match despite being injured, they would inform their audience. But Sid was never allowed to pass on that he knew a player was drunk, even when it was clearly affecting their performance.

It's understandable why. Drink is part of the sport. Most players learn the game at the pub and have a couple of pints as they play. As they move up, the standard improves, but they still rely on a few beers beforehand to reach the optimum state. One current player once told Sid his problem was that he didn't know how much to drink: too little and he was too nervous to play; too much and he was too pissed. Most players know how much they can drink and stay within those limits. A few go too far, either because their match is on late or they play twice in one day and are 'prepared' for the first match but blotto for the second. I can think of one recent major tournament final where a top player lost because by the end of the match he was too drunk to throw anywhere near his best.

During the 1980s, if Sid had mentioned each time a player was drunk, he might have done it every other match. The game is changing now. Most players still take a drink or two before but no more, and an increasing number don't drink before or even at all: Gary Anderson and Justin Pipe to name just two. It can still be an issue in the ranks. There is also an irony when players are banned, as Robbie Green once was, for testing positive for cannabis, yet players can take the stage with veins filled with lager.

That 1987 Embassy was memorable for the final, where John Lowe beat his nemesis Bristow in a seesaw final, 6–4. Back at the hotel afterwards, he was so chuffed that he bought the whole bar champagne, and we were allowed a glass. My first alcoholic drink at the darts. We toasted Lowe and the falling snow, which put our drive back to Leeds the next day in danger. I couldn't imagine anywhere else I would rather be snowed in. Sid was in high spirits, even though Green had been commentating at the end, and this time we had steered clear of the blue movies. Unfortunately, my dream of a never-ending darts trip was thwarted when the snow turned to rain overnight.

We had also been to the Crucible to watch the snooker. Sid had briefly been seconded to Nick Hunter and the sports department in the late 1970s but was useless at the minutiae of the job and was soon sent back to the children's department at the BBC. But he took Glen and me to Sheffield, where we met Jimmy White and hung out backstage with Jack Karnehm and Ted Lowe. It was good fun but not the same as the darts. For a start, it was too near home, so we didn't need to stay overnight, which meant no hanging out in the hotel bar. Part of the whole appeal of the darts was to be among the players and officials and risk death in minibuses driven by drunken stars.

In October 1987, my darting horizons were broadened when I took in the Unipart British Professional Championship in Redcar. My date for this one was Richard Damms, a teammate of mine in the Yorkshire under-15 cricket side. He came from Barnsley and had an accent so thick it made Sid sound like Sue Lawley. And he loved his darts.

It was a well-balanced friendship. He played me *The Queen Is Dead* by the Smiths for the first time; I introduced him to *Viz*. Initially, we didn't like each other, but we bonded on a Yorkshire tour of London and the South, where we shared a room and talked late into the night about music, girls and darts. Dammsy was less worldly than even a Northern oik like me, but he looked older. On the last night of the tour, pissed off at his harsh treatment by the Yorkshire schools coaching team, in an act of defiance he had gone to the off-licence to buy cans of beer, which we supped. There I promised to take him to the darts in Redcar.

He lapped up every bit of it. On the Friday night in Middlesbrough, we went for a Chinese meal: his first ever. Lemon chicken. It gave him the runs. Either that or the Cadbury Boosts we'd eaten all day for reasons we still can't fathom. We shopped for albums. We bought Then Jerico's. It was a rare lapse in taste.

The final was at teatime in a leisure centre in Redcar, but that makes it sound more glamorous than it was. Dammsy spotted a couple of local lasses.

'Reckon I'll chat them up,' he said.

I left him to it. My dating career had been confined to a short-lived fling with Alison Shepherd, who dumped me when my best mate dumped her best mate. Dammsy returned with the two girls and fell into deep chat with one. I sat there tongue-tied and ramrod rigid beside the other. Sid arrived with a huge grin on his face, which soon turned to consternation. Dammsy was waxing lyrical, the girl entranced and amused; attaboy, Sid's face said. I had no chat. Nothing. The lass next to me gazed longingly at Dammsy, while Sid stared at me reproachfully. She got up to leave. Out of solidarity, Dammsy binned his date.

'You've got to work on your patter, son,' warned Sid, grave-faced. Great, I thought, bollocked by my dad for being crap at chatting up a girl.

Dammsy had bought us beer, and Sid didn't seem bothered. 'Can we go to the pub after?' I asked him.

'Why not?' he said. 'Be back here an hour after the final finishes.'

Dammsy sat enraptured by Keith Deller and Leighton Rees, two blasts from the past rediscovering their form, while I counted down the legs and sets until we could experience the delights of Redcar on a Saturday night.

Deller won. I dragged Dammsy out of the door before he had lifted the trophy. Redcar was awash with beer and men, no place for a couple of fifteen-year-old lads. We ummed and aaahed outside a series of garish neon-lit bars, wondering if we would get served. Finally, we found one that let us in. After a couple of beers, we went to an amusement arcade. A lad was staggering around with a deep cut in his head.

'What's up wi thee, bud?' Dammsy asked.

'I've been glassed,' he said.

'Tha wants to get thissen to hospital,' Dammsy replied.

We took it as a sign to go back to the venue and ride Tony

Green's silver Mercedes back to the hotel with Sid, where the post-tournament party was just getting started.

The next morning, we waited for the lift. Martin Fitzmaurice, approximately twenty-five stone, and Leighton Rees, approx. twenty stone, joined us, Dammsy trying not to stare at Leighton with too obvious awe. Nothing was said. Rees farted, and we nearly corpsed. The lift arrived with a ping. The four of us got in, though it was a tight squeeze. Rees asked if we wanted the ground floor. We nodded, praying there would be no farting in an enclosed space. The doors closed.

Then they opened. Rees pressed the button again. The doors closed. Then reopened. This carried on for a while. Then it became clear. It was overloaded. The lift could hold six ordinary people but only two large darts officials or players.

'You two fat bastards better get out,' Fitzmaurice said.

I doubt we weighed a quarter of what they did dripping wet. But we stepped out. The doors closed behind us, the lift descended, and we took the stairs.

Embassy Girl

BY NOW MY face was known by some at the darts: some players, officials, broadcasters and the Embassy 'girls' Sid was so keen for us to meet. One of these women, whose job it was to promote the sponsors, was extremely beautiful, and I and many others were smitten with her. The sponsors' room at Lakeside was a dressing room, and the bath in the en suite was filled to the brim with packs and packs of cigarettes. Sherry, as she was called, caught me leaving with about twenty-eight cartons stuffed in my pockets, in my jumper and down my trousers. She just laughed and said that next time, I should take without feeling the need to hide.

One evening at the bar she deigned to talk to me, and we spent half an hour in conversation, with Sid and the others nudging and winking from across the room. There was clear pride in his eyes after my disastrous showing in Redcar. I didn't feel the need to tell him that she was talking to me about her troubles with her boyfriend.

The next day, as we prepared to leave, he came up to me.

'I asked Sherry out for you,' he said.

'What?!'

'She said you're a lovely lad, but she has a boyfriend.'

He put his hand on my shoulder and furrowed his brow in sympathy. 'Never mind, kidda. Plenty more fish and all that bollocks.'

I was too speechless to tell him I knew she had a boyfriend. And he knew I had a girlfriend.

She had also told me she was twenty-four.

I was sixteen years old.

Before the Fall

WHEN FUTURE HISTORIANS come to write about the evolution of darts, as they surely will, the period between 1988 and 1994 will be viewed as the start of the fall of the empire, the last days of light before a dark age devoid of reasoning and rational thought. From being the smart young buck everyone wanted to meet, it became the shabby loser everyone wanted to ignore. The first warning sign came in 1985, when ITV took *World of Sport* off air, depriving viewers of both Cliff Lazarenko from Hampshire and cliff diving from Acapulco. But 1988 was cataclysmic. First the BBC announced they wouldn't screen another British Professional Championship after that year, reducing their TV tournaments to one and forcing the tournament out of existence; then ITV announced they would not be screening any more darts *at all*. This meant no World Matchplay, no World Masters, not even any of the tournaments screened on regional television, which added valuable pennies and exposure for the pros.

The story is that ITV was seeking to attract affluent, aspirational men and women with money to burn in order to keep advertisers sweet, rather than the drink-soaked working classes they imagined watching darts, who spent all their disposable income on booze and fags. It seemed a short-sighted decision then and more so now when affluent, aspirational men and women flock to arenas to watch darts at £40 a pop, but then the brand has changed.

Sid directed the blame for this decision at Greg Dyke, then director of programmes at ITV, and nursed a grievance against him for appearing to sneer at darts and its fans behind a well-cultivated, mockney man-of-the-people act, in his opinion.

Darts reacted to this crisis with the same equanimity that causes middle-aged men to buy motorbikes. First, in 1989, they banned drinking on stage; then they banned smoking; then, perhaps most shocking of all, they turned the set at Lakeside a shade of pink best described as 'seventies bedspread'. Just like those men racing through the streets in leather to recapture their youth, it didn't work and it looked stupid.

Despite this angst behind the scenes, for us, by which I mean Sid's family and friends, these were the best days of darts watching. Every year without fail, we would make the pilgrimage to Lakeside for a weekend of drinking and darts. The rancour that was gathering like a storm and would rip the game asunder was making Sid's job increasingly less fun, but as soon as he saw us his mood would improve.

The growing problems were also well hidden. Anyone going to Lakeside in those years would have believed the sport to be in rude health. The standard of darts was great, the venue was always sold out and the crowd boisterous but good-natured – and thirsty. It was during this time that my stepbrother Nick was at the bar and overheard one man ask for sixty-four pints of lager. The barmaid blanched. 'It's all right,' he explained.

'There's eight of us.' Sid shamelessly stole this story and adapted it for his own ends, often attributing it to the crowd at the Irish Centre in Leeds for *The Indoor League*.

We joined in the drinking, with sometimes disastrous consequences. In 1990, my best friend Jason and I had spent the whole afternoon and evening on the beer, so when play ended we were as drunk as two seventeen-year-olds could be while remaining upright. By now, Bob Potter had built a hotel on the same site as the Lakeside, so drunken darts players could stagger home across the car park rather than commandeer minibuses and endanger innocent women and children. Within a few minutes of Bruce Spendley or Freddie Williams calling the last 'Game, shot and the match' of the night, the darters, scorers, broadcasters and hangers-on reconvened to a private room where a cabaret ensued, darts matches were played and many, many drinks were sunk.

Jason and I lurched in and found the pool table free. After a few frames, Eric Bristow and his driver swaggered over.

'Fancy a game, lads?'

We certainly weren't going to turn down a chance to play the greatest darts player in the world, so we agreed. We ordered another pint, and we beat them easily.

'Fancy making it more interesting, lads?' Eric asked.

'Yeah right, Eric. I've seen you annihilate countless players on the dartboard. There has been no better player under pressure than you. You played money matches for a living as a teenager and know exactly what's required to win. You've spent your whole life in pubs and bars playing pool and snooker, whereas I won't be legally old enough to enter a pub for another five months. Not only that, you appear to be sober whereas me and my mate are now so pissed we can barely find our own balls with our hands, never mind see the ones on the table.'

That's what I should've said. Instead, Jason and I looked at each other, nodded eagerly and said, 'Sure.'

'Tenner?'

We nodded even more enthusiastically. As he was always willing to do, Sid had handed me a wad of cash earlier that evening to keep Jason and me lubricated. Sid was always a soft touch for money, unlike Rene, who wanted reasons, a cost breakdown and wondered where all your pocket money had gone before saying 'No.' If you asked Sid for some money, you inevitably got it. If you said you were going to spend it at the pub, you got more. 'Make sure you get a round in,' he'd say, reaching into his back pocket where he had more crisp tenners than Jim Bowen.

So this was a chance to earn some cash and pay our own way, rather than having to go cap in hand to him. We broke off, a red went in, I potted one more and missed a tricky long shot. A decent start.

Jason didn't get to play a shot. Eric cleaned up at his first visit.

'Another one, lads?'

'Nah, we're right,' we said, lesson learned.

Except we didn't learn. We played again. And three more frames after that, in which we potted a total of one ball.

Sid wandered over, perhaps sensing danger. I had £10 in my pocket.

'Dad, you owe Eric £50.'

He knew instantly what had happened. I can't remember if Eric took the cash or not when he realized Sid would be coughing up – he probably did, given that it would be teaching us a lesson. But Sid was as angry with me as I'd seen him since the blue-movie debacle.

'What sort of prat thinks they can hustle Eric Bristow?' he hissed.

The next day he gave me no money for beer.

~

The post-match cabaret always stretched long into the night, and Sid was often at the microphone leading the sing-song. At one championship, when I decided rather unwisely for my liver to spend three nights at the darts, on the Thursday he and I called it a night at a reasonably sensible hour and went back to his room.

As we arrived, he turned on his heel.

'Hang on, I'll be back in a minute,' he explained.

I went out on to the balcony to smoke a last cigarette. The air was cold and dry, and the night as black as ink; the lights from the rooms made shimmering diamonds on the surface of the oily-looking lake. The noise from the cabaret hung in the frigid air: the plink of a Bontempi organ and a crooning male voice. A Geordie voice. My dad's voice. He was singing 'Your Cheatin' Heart'. The song ended, there was the sound of applause and thirty seconds later he was walking in the room.

'Sorry, kidda, I'd forgotten something,' he explained.

I wish I'd been in the bedroom the following year when Sid was at the mic. A group of BBC staffers had chosen to sing 'The Most Beautiful Girl In The World' by Charlie Rich, though assault might be a better description. They swiftly lost the room and were about to get the hook, in favour of Jocky Wilson's incomprehensible but moving rendition of 'Danny Boy', which he reimagined as a torchsong, or perhaps John Lowe's cracked, plaintive version of 'Wonderful Tonight' by Clapton, when Sid went to the rescue. He did this not by joining in or adapting the lyrics in comic fashion; instead, for inexplicable reasons, he stripped down to his baggy blue Y-fronts. I was sitting with my uncle Derrick. All the booze in the world couldn't take the sting from the embarrassment.

'That's my dad,' I winced.

'That's my brother,' he cringed.

This happened year after year, most nights. One Friday night I didn't go to bed but spent it carousing with the Merseyside Darts Organisation, crooning out Beatles songs with Kevin Kenny (as a Liverpool fan, a player bearing the names of the club's two greatest strikers and my favourite players was always going to be a hero) and joining a massed singalong to 'In My Liverpool Home'.

The next morning, Sid surveyed my shell-shocked state in the bar as he came down for breakfast.

'What happened?'

The only thing I could remember was that Liverpool had two cathedrals.

Later that morning, after two hours' sleep and a shower, I went back to the bar. Dougie Donnelly was interviewing Phil Taylor and Mike Gregory ahead of the final. Uncle Derrick and Robbie and pals were playing Sid at pool in a side room and waved me over. I walked towards what looked like an open door but was actually a glass window, and I hit it headfirst. Thankfully, it didn't break, but the crash halted the interview and Sid didn't stop laughing for weeks. From that point on I wasn't Dan or Sid's son, but, in Eric's words, the muppet who walked into a window.

~

In all this, Sid's greatest achievement wasn't his commentary but smuggling us into his hotel room. One year, seven of us slept in there, of whom only my dad was supposed to. That was the night before the final, when everyone had been drinking until 4 a.m. You could have cut the air in the room with a spoon. At 9 a.m., the phone rang and was passed along the bed from Uncle Derrick to his mate Ritchie Stafford to Sid, who had slept between him and Nick. I was on the floor together with Nick's mate Dave and my friend Jason.

'Allo,' said Sid, voice ravaged, rasping and dry. 'OK. Oh right,' he said.

He put his hand on the receiver.

'Can you bastards keep quiet? I'm about to be interviewed live on BBC radio by Cliff Morgan.'

He stopped to cough and spit.

'Hi, Cliff, how you doing?' he said.

For the next two minutes, he managed to avoid giving the impression that he had drunk enough to float a fleet the night before and had only had a few hours' comatose sleep between the farting, snoring corpses of six other drunks. I knew then he had become a real pro.

Occasionally, people had to improvise and other times beds found them rather than vice versa. One evening, Nick's mate Dave had enjoyed himself too liberally at the darts, and as we made our way back to the hotel, he staggered off the wrong way around the lake. A search party had been sent to find him, but it was too dark and cold, and, anyway, the cabaret had started. If he had fallen to an icy death, then he wouldn't want us to miss out on valuable drinking time.

The next morning, cue Sid's bedroom, and among the casualties strewn across the floor was Dave. He couldn't remember what had happened.

'I had this really weird dream last night,' he said to us. 'I dreamt I slept with Tony Green.'

We all laughed and took the piss out of his inability to hold his ale.

There was a knock on the door. Sid answered. Tony Green. He had the commentary rota in his hand.

'Here, Sid,' he said, pointing to the yellow piece of paper. 'I thought maybe you'd do the first part of the final and I'll do the second.'

Sid was hungover and wasn't in the mood to discuss it. He nodded. 'OK, kidda.'

'Great. I'll tell Keith. I'll see you later.'

He turned to Dave's skinny body on the floor. 'But you, you bastard, you can have your fucking watch back!'

He threw Dave's watch at him.

It wasn't a dream. Dave's homing instinct had drawn him back to the hotel, not to our room but Tony Green's opposite. It was unlocked and empty, so he went in and slid into bed. Only to be kicked out a few hours later when Tony's card game ended.

'He could've at least asked for my number,' said Dave gloomily.

The End of Childhood

MY BOND WITH Lynemouth loosened when I became a teenager and eating tea and toast in front of a roaring fire seemed less thrilling than hanging out with my mates, or playing football or cricket in Pudsey. There was one visit with Sid when I was fifteen, and I was more interested in sneaking a pint in the Hot L than I was in sitting with my granddad. There was a chasm between us when once we had been so close. Bob knew it too. 'I don't think I'll ever see your snooker table,' he said mournfully, referring to a Christmas present I had been given several years earlier.

He never did. I don't think I saw him again. In November 1989, he was taken into hospital with breathing problems, caused by his worsening angina, where he died a day later aged eighty-three. His funeral was the gravest day of my short life. Martha had asked that my cousin Robbie and I should help carry the coffin. My uncle Derrick prepared us for it by giving us shots of Scotch, which might have steadied my nerves but did nothing for my legs. As pallbearers, we walked in front of the hearse along Dalton Avenue, the nagging east wind biting into my core. Then came the surreal, backbreaking walk into the church with the coffin cutting into my shoulder. I held up until I had to lower his coffin into the ground at the cemetery. Martha stepped forward with a red rose, which she asked Derrick and Sid to kiss, before she threw it into the grave with her husband. Then I melted into tears, realizing that sunny childhood days do come to an end, as do the people you love.

Back at Dalton Avenue, his worn maroon armchair lay empty as a mark of respect as we all hit the booze hard. The Irish priest who had conducted the Requiem Mass joined us and eyed a bottle of wine in Derrick's hand.

'Would there be anything left in that bottle?' he asked.

'Aye. A canny bit,' Derrick replied.

'Praise the Lord,' said the priest and offered forth his glass.

Later that day, we decamped to the Hot L, where we got smashed. Or at least I did. I remember being driven away from Lynemouth that evening in a haze of booze and tears. From that point on, I would return only for funerals. A place I had once associated only with life was now indelibly linked with death.

Derrick went first, to everyone's grief but no one's surprise. After leaving the RAF, he had returned to Lynemouth, where he slept at Martha's but lived in the Hot L. The pair bickered constantly, and Sid would often travel up there to keep the peace. Inevitably, he'd join Derrick in the pub and get roaring pissed with him, and then return home full of booze and remorse and foreboding that his brother was drinking himself to death.

He was right, but there was nothing much that could be done about it. Derrick had set a course, and it was one of self-destruction. He went to the pub every lunchtime and evening, and grimly chewed his way through a dozen or so pints. His mood grew increasingly dark the worse his spiral became. The humour and mischievous wit had been dulled, replaced with bitterness and sullenness. My dad tried to give him money, set him up in business, but it was no use. He wanted to drink, and it seems he wanted to die.

After several years of alcoholism, in 1996 his liver downed tools and he was admitted to hospital. One evening, like a homing pigeon, he walked out of the hospital in his pyjamas and dressing gown and strolled two miles from Ashington to Lynemouth and the Hot L. News of his hospitalization had spread fast, and the locals were amazed to see him walk in. They persuaded him to have an orange juice and someone drove him back, and it seemed that this might be the warning sign he needed to get help and treatment. Sid went to visit him, and all seemed well. Then four days later he died suddenly. He was forty-eight.

So yet again Robbie and I were walking down Dalton Avenue in front of a hearse. Once again we staggered under the weight of a coffin, though this time it was his dad's. Sid gave a moving eulogy in praise of his brother's wit: 'Jungle Fighter' he called him, a reference to when he was stationed in Belize with the RAF, even though the most dangerous thing he faced was falling coconuts.

Afterwards, we headed for the pub, where the landlord bought us all drinks on the house in memory of his best customer. Martha was never one to refuse a trip to the boozer, but she did that day, blaming the pub for selling Derrick the drink that killed him rather than Derrick for drinking it.

I could tell it crushed Sid. Derrick was the only man who

could match the speed of his wit, even if he couldn't remotely match the capacity of his brain. The pair of them revelled in each other's humour. My dad felt responsible for Derrick, just as he had when they were kids. He felt he had failed him. He felt guilty for standing him round after round when it was clear his alcoholism was worsening. And he felt guilty for the success and stability that he had finally achieved and which always eluded Derrick. Sid had scaled heights that Derrick could only dream of. To be fair, he didn't try. He wanted to forge his own path. But ultimately it was one that had led nowhere.

Robbie moved up to Lynemouth and in with Martha. She died in 1998. Until the end, she downed the gin and smoked a stream of tabs. She was taken into hospital with breathing problems but still managed to have an occasional cigarette when someone helped her outside the front door where she sat, huddled up in her pink anorak, and smoked a couple of tabs before the cold forced her back inside. She returned home, but it was clear she wouldn't be able to manage. She entered a care home, where every effort was made to make her comfortable. She toddled around with a Zimmer frame, a carrier bag hanging off one of the handles with her Silk Cut 100s in it, and socialized with a couple of people she knew who were also in there. But the light went out of her eyes. She wouldn't have any of the precious family pictures from home in her room, only, for some bizarre reason, a photograph of Princess Diana. She refused to have flowers and sent them to the communal rooms when anyone brought them for her. Dad and Robbie would take her out to the pub down the road where she would nurse a gin and tonic and eat a prawn sandwich. But she was not getting any better. On my dad's last visit, she was too weak to hold her own cigarette. But rather than stopping smoking, she asked him to hold it for her. A stubborn woman, Martha.

My auntie Iris called me one morning to tell me that she had died. Sid was in the USA with Irene, and I broke the news. The connection with Lynemouth was broken for good, for us all.

Robbie and his younger sister Regan felt the break as keenly as me, if not more. When Derrick and their mum Iris split up, they spent even more time in Lynemouth than I did, much to my seething envy. Whole summer holidays, not just the occasional week. Robbie was an adventurous, open and gentle soul who was there so often he'd made friends with some local lads, which I never did. One Christmas – they got to spend Christmas and New Year there, the bastards! – the weather turned bad, and Robbie was unable to travel back home to Suffolk, so he was enrolled in the local primary school for a week. I didn't so much envy that as the chance of a few extra stolen days in Dalton Avenue.

Robbie died suddenly, heartbreakingly, at the age of twenty-nine. At his funeral, they played 'Run For Home' by Lindisfarne. It was his, Iris and Regan's song, summing up their feelings towards Lynemouth and the North-East and the warmth of Dalton Avenue. As a self-confessed musical snob who spent much of his later teenage and student years going to see the likes of the Throwing Muses and Nick Cave on his own because he had no other mates who liked them, Lindisfarne were hairy, folky anathema to me. I knew them only for that song they sang with Gazza in his fake-boobs, beery and teary period of fame, about sickly sausage rolls and the Fog on the Tyne. I'd never heard 'Run For Home', but the song's simple, honest sentimentality hit me in the gut like a punch, and as the tears rolled down my face, the years rolled away and I was back in the car, my head lolling against the window as I watched the distant fires flare in the sky, kittenish with excitement at going to Dalton Avenue, or curling slowly across the Tyne on a train into Newcastle station with my heart in my mouth, or turning on to Bridge Road past the Hot L, or in the front room beneath the Lincrusta and polished plates in front of a roaring fire, biting my toast and then quickly taking a sip of tea as my granddad always did . . .

Poisoned Arrows

S ID, MY STEPBROTHER Nick and I often referred to the calamitous and acrimonious split in darts as 'the Schism'. It was a joke, of course, and one whose ludicrousness appealed to Sid. But it also contained great truth: the divide was so absolute that only a reference to religious argument did it justice. There were heretics (the players), those who were accused of being schismatics (managers and agents), and eventually a new church emerged (the World Darts Council – WDC – later the Professional Darts Corporation – PDC). Blood was not shed, but lifelong friendships were ended and long-lived enmities started. There were court cases, rancorous argument and years and years of name-calling.

No other sport has experienced a dispute as bitter or as prolonged. Kerry Packer's breakaway World Series Cricket is often mentioned in comparison, but it was brief and the existing powers realized there was no way to compete, so they chose to accommodate. Not so in darts. The British Darts Organisation (BDO) ignored the WDC for years. Then, when the WDC's power usurped their own, they chose denial and simply refused to accept defeat. The war was over, yet BDO officials chose to keep patrolling the jungle like lost Japanese soldiers refusing to surrender.

The origins of the split lay in the sport's televised birth. In order to find the players to contest a tournament, the organizers turned to BDO head Olly Croft. It was an opportunity he seized. Not only did he help ensure the success of those early World Championships but it cemented him and his organization as the dominant force in the game. Other bodies were simply squeezed out of existence. By the early 1980s, the BDO had total control of British darts. They were in charge of super league darts, county darts, major tournaments and the World Championships, and, as a founder member of the World Darts Federation, where they had terrific influence, a major say in international darts. It was root-to-branch, point-to-flight dominance.

During the boom years of the early 1980s, as darts' profile rose, more players turned professional and their exhibition bookings and incomes grew, few people minded that the BDO had such a grip on all parts of the game. People were understandably indebted to Croft and his relentless work on their behalf. The broadcasters were happy with the product, while sponsors lined up to lend their name to the sport. In truth, it was easy for the BDO: people came to them.

But while people were happy with how Croft had helped drive the darts boom, there were a few siren voices who were alarmed at how centralized power had become. One of them was Dick Allix, Eric Bristow's manager, an urbane and laconic musician turned impresario. He and others, notably John Lowe, believed the players should form their own body to represent their concerns, and so the Professional Darts Players Association came into being. They tried to arrange a meeting to discuss ideas with the BDO, but the BDO were never keen to sit down with them and refused to recognize the organization. Alarm bells started to ring.

This autocratic approach continued, and while the sun was shining, the few dissenting voices were ignored. But as the game's popularity started to dwindle in the late 1980s, TV tournaments disappeared and sponsors with them, and, crucially, this meant reduced exposure for the players, which led to fewer exhibition bookings and less income. Discontent started to grow.

The players believed they had been pivotal in the sport's rise and wanted a say in how to reverse its fall. The BDO felt that as they had been responsible for the sport's popularity, they also deserved the players' gratitude, and there was no fall, just a fallow period, and the good times would return. In the meantime, they had the wider sport to look after, not just a group of professionals. And on and on it went in ever more circular arguments. These started in the mid eighties, grew more discordant as the decade wore on, and by the 1990s, when only the Embassy was shown on TV, they had become poisonous. Gangs and factions were everywhere: the professional players, the managers, the officials, and those in between, which included Sid. He had no gang. We were it. When we came to those early 1990s tournaments, he embraced us eagerly, a cheery respite from the growing animosity and disquiet otherwise simmering beneath the surface. The cabaret still played, everyone still mingled, but something was in the air, and it wasn't just Sid's hammy singing.

As the dispute intensified, Sid was genuinely torn, like a child upset at squabbling parents. He loved some of the players: without their swagger and character he would never have been able to carve a niche for himself as their chronicler and cheerleader. His proximity to them over more than a decade also meant he counted many as friends; he understood their concerns. As he was also seeing his commentary income dwindle, he felt for them too. But he had another job to fall back on; they didn't.

Yet he also admired Croft for his chutzpah and cockiness. Sid was no businessman, far from it, but he knew an operator when he saw one. He often joked that Olly's trumpeted claim of a 'darts family' had a mafioso ring to it, but he admired how Croft had called him to tell him his players on *The Indoor League* were crap and then shown similar enterprise in turning the sport into a popular international game. He never drank and sang with Olly and his crew like he did with the players, but he held a genuine affection for both him, his formidable wife Lorna and the other officials.

But the difficulties of being a push-me pull-you in his sport's internecine struggle had only just begun. It all came to a head in 1992, leading to two turbulent years for all involved, not least Sid.

$\sim$

In January 1992, sixteen of the world's leading darters, including world champions Eric Bristow, John Lowe, Keith Deller, Phil Taylor, Jocky Wilson and Dennis Priestley, announced the formation of the World Darts Council. But Sid was distracted by more troubling news. In April that year, he was made redundant from the BBC.

He sank into a slump. At fifty-one, he felt washed up. His career as a TV producer was at an end, and his sinecure as a darts commentator, which brought him acclaim and fed his ego, was in jeopardy. For a few months, he wallowed in self-pity, but with Irene's support and some cajoling from the rest of us, he started to think seriously about a freelance career. A production company based in Newcastle suggested he front a light-hearted programme for Tyne Tees where he spent time as a student and a butler and holidayed at a caravan park. It's fair to say *Waddell's World* wasn't in line to win many BAFTAs when it was screened in 1993 – Sid was always stilted and unnatural in front of the camera, in contrast to his fluid articulacy behind it – but the programme helped rebuild his confidence, even if the sight of him swilling snakebite in a student nightclub wearing Dr Marten boots, combat trousers, lumberjack shirt and donkey jacket was an image some members of his family found difficult to shake.

In darts, the endgame was nigh. The WDC organized its first ever tournament, the Lada Classic, screened on Anglia Television from a nightclub in Norwich in October 1992. But the tournament did nothing to improve relations between the two warring bodies at the 1993 Embassy, darts' equivalent of Gettysburg, Orgreave and the St Scholastica Day Riot all rolled into one. The WDC were keen to show the world and the BBC that there was a new organization in town and to wear their logo on their shirts: their darts on their sleeves. The BDO countered by ordering them to take them off; this was their tournament, always had been, and they should be removed. A stand-off ensued.

After lengthy talks with the BDO and the BBC, a

compromise was reached. The rebel players decided to remove the offending badges and save their energies for battles to come. But the redoubtable Tommy Cox, manager of Jocky Wilson, and Bristow's manager Dick Allix, both directors of the WDC, and the players had finally had enough: that would be the last time they would let the BDO order them around. They held a momentous press conference, with the Rose and Thistle in Frimley Green doubling as the Appomattox Courthouse, and issued an ultimatum: their players would not take part in the next World Championship unless the tournament was under WDC control.

I followed all this remotely from Pudsey, with Sid relaying the grim news from the front by phone. I was mortified at what it meant. The sport I had come to know so well was tearing itself apart. Yes, I loved the weekends at Lakeside and dreaded their end: it was the highlight of my year. A chance to spend time with Sid, to sing and drink and revel in the whole ribald, bacchanalian show. But more than that I cared for those caught in the crossfire. The BDO will come to their senses, I thought. Surely the pride of its officials was not more important than the game?

Sid was asked to discuss the dispute on screen with Dougie Donnelly. He said the BDO should be more democratic and allow the players a greater say, but that the WDC's statement had been too aggressive and provocative, and their demand to control the next World Championship too far-reaching. The result of his attempt to play Pontius Pilate was that he was crucified: the BDO did not take kindly to criticism from a man who they believed was part of the 'family', while Tommy Cox gave him a gobful because Sid in his new-found position as a freelance producer was in the process of helping them organize and screen a competition on Tyne Tees in the spring of 1993, and yet here he was roasting them live on the BBC.

When we arrived, he embraced us warmly. There were factions and groups everywhere, muttering darkly. Sid was happy to have his gang with him. The week, he said, had been hellish. Despite the turmoil, he had still produced inspired commentary. Steve Beaton, young, well-built with a wet-look permed mullet and porn star 'tache, had ripped through the field. 'He's not Adonis,' Sid said. 'He's *the* Donis.' Meanwhile, he got rather more sleep before the final than usual, because Derrick and his five mates slept in a Transit van in the car park, though Sid still smuggled them all in for breakfast.

The final of the last ever unified World Darts Championship was a disappointment. Ironically, two of the rebel players contested the final, John Lowe and Alan Warriner, with Stoneface (Lowe) claiming his third title. The next year, the champion would not be back to defend his trophy.

∽

In April, my mate Jason and I went up to Newcastle to join the darts revolutionaries in their latest crusade: the Samson Classic, staged by the WDC, screened by Tyne Tees, producer and commentator S. Waddell. But it didn't feel like a new dawn. It was held in a television studio and had all the atmosphere of a morning Mass. In such a frigid setting, the players looked uncomfortable, glancing hopefully at the audience for a drunken or even slightly tipsy roar or cheer that might ignite their darts. But there was no bar, only waitress service, obtained by pre-paid tickets to circumvent the licensing laws, and everyone was sober.

Jason and I had also fallen foul of the new WDC rules to improve the game's image. Not only must the players be smart but the crowd too: no jeans or trainers. Jason and I were wearing both, not anticipating that the tournament officials would try to invoke the dress code of a provincial nightclub. We were allowed in the first night, but the next evening we each had to wear a pair of my dad's trousers. We were both at least four inches taller than him. How walking in with a pair of slacks at half-mast like Beppo the Clown improved the image of darts was unclear, but we were not going to argue with Tommy Cox.

In the pub beforehand, as the players and their officials 'warmed up', the talk was of little other than darts politics. From moles in the enemy camp, the word was that the BDO were on the verge of banning the rebel players from all darts, including county matches, and that any BDO players *and officials* who played with or against the rebels in an exhibition or associated with their activities would also be banned, thus weaving the split into the fabric of the game. Players who had played against each other and together for years were forced apart, friendships were ruined and ended as people were made to take sides, and acrimony became the norm in a game previously known for its harmony.

Those present were putting a brave face on it all, but these were dark times, and the stress was telling. The rumour turned out to be true. The BDO ratified their proposals in late April, and the rebels were cast into the darting wilderness, able to play only amongst themselves, their future uncertain. Most remained strong and resolute; a few wobbled and experienced long dark nights of the soul. Cracks appeared: Mike Gregory and Chris Johns eventually relented later that year and rejoined the BDO.

The first glimmer of hope for the rebels in those dark tumultuous months of 1993 was the offer from Sky to televise their first World Championship starting on Boxing Day and finishing on 2 January, mischievously and ingeniously scheduled so its winner was declared before the Embassy started. Skol agreed to sponsor the event, and to augment the fourteen rebels minus Johns and Gregory the field was padded out with two Englishmen, Graeme Stoddart and Kevin Burrows, brave enough to defy the threats and strictures of the BDO and throw in their lot with the rebels, as well as a genial Irishman named Tom Kirby and seven American players, who were only there because the USA was one of the three nations in the World Darts Federation who refused to implement the BDO ban worldwide, stating such restrictions of freedom were inimical to their nation's beliefs.

The rebels faced no choice other than to launch legal proceedings to overturn the ban, arguing it was an illegal restraint of trade. The case would run for the next four years and cost huge sums of money. A number of rebel officials and players donated their own money to fund the suit, some even remortgaging their houses. If the rebels lost, they would be in ruins, financially and structurally. They would not be able to continue. But even in the face of such stakes, folding was not an option.

On Boxing Day, Sid and I took our turkey-bloated bodies to the Railway Pub to watch the inaugural WDC World Darts Championship. We sat sipping pints as the Sky coverage unfolded: gaudy lights, dry ice, pounding rock music announcing the players, who were accompanied, like boxers, by young women – it made the plush fuchsia stage at Lakeside seem genteel. The way Sid went on to tell the story, he was immediately stricken by jealousy. The next week, he would be at Lakeside for the BBC, chronicling a tournament with no stars, no razzmatazz, where he would be made unwelcome because of his associations with the rebels, and he longed to join this revolution, with its snappy, snazzy coverage, and to be back with his mates.

There is some truth in it. His heart was with the players, and he would have liked to have been sitting alongside his mate Dave Lanning in the commentary box for the first time. But the queasy look on a few players' faces betrayed their insecurity about this new dawn, and Sid was occasionally scathing about some of the players brought in to make up the numbers. Rather than being bewitched by the Sky coverage, as he later claimed, he thought aspects of it over the top.

But in a week or so he would be at Lakeside. Sid was not a man to work in half-measures. So in order to give his best in Frimley Green, he convinced himself the rebel tournament was inferior and that Lakeside had the class and the pedigree. He wrote this out of his future histories, but he even offered a few words of scathing criticism of the rival championship on air, extolling the new breed of darts players given a chance to shine now the 'has-beens' had moved on.

It was all just showbiz though, much like some of his later criticism of the BDO. He was paid to promote a product, and if that meant taking potshots at their rivals in Muswell Hill, Sid was willing to do it. There was so much bad feeling and so many barbs being thrown across the great divide by both sides, who would notice another few bons mots? In my opinion, he often overdid it, especially when it became clear as the years passed that the WDC (particularly in the years after changing its name to the PDC) were winning the propaganda war and the BDO was in irreversible decline. Then it seemed unnecessary. The point was being made emphatically on the dartboard and on people's screens. There was no need for Sid to gloat. But, as he argued, many people had sacrificed so much to ensure the success of the WDC/PDC they had a right to brag, and as the voice of the game he was merely reflecting that.

The 1994 Embassy was a strange affair. We went and had our fun, but the darts had palled, like being at a party after the beautiful people had left (perhaps the only time Eric et al might be referred to as the beautiful people). The last remaining eighties great, Bobby George, did what he could to inject colour, and his run to the final offered a satisfying narrative arc. The winner, John Part, would go on to prove himself a worthy world champion and a great of the game, but at the time it had the feel of the 1980 Moscow Olympics after the US boycott, or Test cricket during Packer's World Series: the best players and most enthralling characters in the game weren't there, so the whole event felt hollow and fraudulent. I believed darts could not survive the split: the result had been two disappointing World Championships rather than one good one. Surely they reunited or the sport died?

Thankfully, my predictions have always proved to be as accurate as my old man's.

Manningham Mills

IT WAS THE end of the 1989 cricket season, and my team Bowling Old Lane, affectionately known as Dog Shit Alley, had been playing at Manningham Mills. We had lost and been relegated, but the beer and the bonhomie were flowing as we shared one last evening together before a long winter without cricket. Sid decided to mark the occasion with a song . . .

He loved to sing, and it wasn't simply confined to the Lakeside cabaret. I suspect that deep down he'd not quite scratched the itch that made him form the Gravyboatmen. He would have loved to have been a rock star. He had the moves; Sid's dancing was legendary. Women queued up to jive with him, while everyone else howled with appreciative laughter at his Elvis leg-wobbles and Jagger-esque strutting (while his son hid behind the fruit machine with embarrassment). Few weddings were complete without Sid taking to the stage to sing 'Ain't That A Shame', where without fail he'd turn his back to the audience, wrap his arms around himself and run them up and down his own back to mimic the wandering hands of a lover, though in reality it looked like what it was – an old man groping himself.

But here was another party piece, and I braced myself for it with some Holsten Pils. To the tune of the scouting song 'The Quartermaster's Store', he went around the entire room replacing the animals ('There were rats, rats, big as alley cats') that populate the titular store with those present in the bar, garnished with some sexual innuendo.

It started off mildly enough. 'There was P.J., P.J., doing it with the D.J.' Before taking a turn for the bawdy. 'There was Martin, Martin, he'd finished before she was startin'.' Then became outright filthy. 'There was Miller, Miller, he could cum but couldn't fill her.' No one was spared, not even Irene. 'There was Rene, Rene, she was cheap but she was clean.'

It was OK. I was eighteen.

But our under-15s' captain and his parents were a bit shocked.

Into the Sky

I WAS IN MY final term at university when the phone call came that I expected but had secretly dreaded. It was Sid; he sounded upbeat, almost jubilant.

'I've signed a contract with Sky, kidda!'

'Fantastic!' I said. I was delighted for him. Particularly as he explained that they were lining up more tournaments to go alongside their World Championship, starting with a World Matchplay in Blackpool that summer. Finally, he would be paid well for the job he performed best and end the uncertainty over his future. It seemed like his career fortunes had been umbilically linked to the darts: success, then decline, severance and then rebirth. He sounded genuinely excited. After the rejection of redundancy, to be courted and headhunted by Sky was the lift his ego needed.

'Can you still do the Embassy?' In my mind, he was hired by the broadcaster, whom neither darts code wanted to anger. If the BBC wanted Sid, he'd be there, and the cabaret of my annual jolly would be secure.

He paused. 'It's an exclusive contract, son. From now on I work for Sky. Sorry.'

I was being churlish and selfish, so I snapped out of it. 'No, it's great news. Can we come to Blackpool?'

'Course you bloody can!'

In early August, Jason and I drove with my university mate Jonny to the jewel of the Fylde coast. Jason and I both knew it well, from childhood trips and boozy teenage nights out. Everywhere you looked, you saw faded glamour and peeling remnants of its Victorian heyday. In the summer, the North flocked there for a week of beer, fried food, bawdy shows and trilling amusement arcades: simple working-class fun. It was the ideal place to host a darts tournament. Jonny, a southern lad from an army family and privately educated, viewed it more as sociology.

We arrived mid afternoon. The darts was being held in the Empress Ballroom of the Winter Gardens, a gilded Victorian pleasure palace festooned with chandeliers and ornate decoration. Every single prime minister since the Second World War had addressed their party's conference here; the Stone Roses had also performed there to their simian-strolling masses. This was a place of real history, and it seeped from its barrel-vaulted ceiling and spring-laden mahogany floor.

Sid was wide-eyed with excitement, thrilled at the chance to commentate with Lanning and Gwynne. At the BBC, he commentated alone, but another mind to bounce ideas off, riff and joke with added another dimension to his commentary, as well as making it more enjoyable. These were early days, but for once he felt part of a gang: him, John and Dave as the Three Musketeers, the Thieves of Badgags, rather than the occasionally testy rivalry he and Tony Green had shared. His director also gave him free rein to indulge himself to the extreme and inject as many rhetorical flourishes as possible. There would be no instructions to calm it down – quite the opposite. The players were also delighted to be reunited with him; they knew Sid gave them kudos, personality, and that his presence would entice quote-thirsty writers and journalists to cover their side of the game.

The hall was only three quarters full, but that was impressive for a warm summer afternoon. The WDC were letting punters in for free during the afternoon sessions, hoping that more would return and pay in the evening. The tactic worked, and the evening session was almost full. Our first experience of Sky's presentation was disorientating for those used to more staid production techniques. It was hard not to giggle when the MC screamed the name of the next player, the lights strobed, music blared, the dry ice billowed and then cleared to reveal . . . a sheepish-looking darts player. But it looked good on TV, the players soon got used to it, and the music had the punters on their feet.

Back at the hotel, the players and officials and broadcasters still had a drink, but there was no singing. This was professional darts; the cabaret was no more, though we did sit at the same table as Duncan Norvelle and the Grumbleweeds, in town for a summer season, so the showbiz vibe lived on. Some players had decided to stay off site to focus on their matches and not on a piss-up after, yet another worrying sign of professionalism. Something had been lost, but, amid the turmoil, the mood of the WDC contingent was optimistic: there could be a future. And Sid had never looked happier.

Between Christmas and New Year, Jason and I went to the World Championship at Purfleet. The Circus Tavern was a nightclub off the A13, in the middle of nowhere. Outside it looked grim and functional, but inside it was hot and hostile; the crowds were close to the stage, almost on top of the players. It was a wonderful venue to watch a game of darts, less one in which to spend a weekend. From then on, my visits to the World Championships were for a night only, purely to watch the darts rather than sing and play with the players, particularly after my move to London in 1997. I still took in a few days of earthy delight at Blackpool every now and then, as well as trips to tournaments in Doncaster and Ireland when the PDC started to host the Grand Prix there. But as a worker and not a loafer there was less chance for darts. Sid always welcomed family and friends. No other broadcaster had his family around, but Sid thrived on it. It was a party he wanted us all to share.

~

During these years, my relationship with him was changing. From that of a father and son, albeit unconventional, it became more equal. As I became a man, dare I say it, I sometimes felt like the father figure, particularly at the darts. If I sensed Sid was about to order a whisky or light a cigar, I was there to warn against it. It's like I was channelling Irene, trying to protect Sid from his own self-inflicted follies. If he was angry with someone, I'd calm him down; if he had a work dilemma, I'd provide advice. At times he sought my approval, not vice versa: he'd quote his lines and check my reaction, and on the rare occasions he messed up or made a mistake he wanted reassurance that everything would be all right. There were times, watching him tie one on or lead a late-night chorus when he should be watching his voice, when I tried vainly to persuade him to rein it in and felt like poor stuffy Saffy in *Absolutely Fabulous*, shaking her head at the excesses of her ageing but adolescent mother and pals.

Many of the happiest days of my dad's career came during those early years with Sky and the WDC, as something special grew. There were setbacks: in 1995, Jocky Wilson did a midnight flit from his house in Whitley Bay to avoid the taxman and scarpered back to the same Kirkcaldy streets he had escaped two decades before. He spent the last years of his life as a recluse, barely leaving his tiny council house, resisting all attempts from Sid and others to show his face and accept some acclaim for his achievements, even a last payday. He was done with darts, his body broken by excessive drinking and smoking. The last time Sid saw him, Jocky told him he still watched it on TV, but he didn't miss it. Sid did not believe a word of it but respected his decision.

~

In 1997, the four-year court case that had paralysed the game ended. There were no real winners or losers unless you count the lawyers who had trousered hundreds of thousands of pounds from each organization. But there was a settlement, and in the cold light of day it was clear the WDC had the spoils. They had to drop the 'World' from their name and so become the Professional Darts Corporation. But more significantly, the BDO were forced to drop their ban. The years of struggle had been worth it. Years of plenty lay ahead.

Sid's Rules OK

A FEW MONTHS AFTER Sid died, I was going through my dad's archive. I say archive, but that makes it sound more official and curated than it was. In reality, it was a pile of papers and notes, newspaper cuttings and tournament programmes from thirty-five years of darts commentary. All of it had been defaced by his scrawl.

His handwriting was runic in its impenetrability. Carved into rock it would make the Rosetta Stone seem like a Janet and John story. But to him it made sense. Everything was recorded – averages, past performances, quirky slices of information about each player – indecipherable to all but him. But it was essential: before each tournament he would sit at the kitchen table in Pudsey and 'go through' his notes. Dave Allen, the Professional Darts Corporation's overworked press officer, would arm him with information about any new players, which he would scrawl in a dog-eared corner of their bio, or on a fresh sheet of A4 if he thought they were going places. Then he would sit and ruminate. God forbid if this ritual was interrupted. My stepmother Irene once opened the back door to take out some washing, creating a draught that sent reams and reams of Sid's papers billowing around the room like confetti.

'Shit!' he screamed, running around, arms flapping, trying to catch them. 'Fu—cking hell!'

As I waded through this pile, recognizing one written word in ten, I found myself drawn to old programmes from tournaments I'd attended as a boy. I'd long since lost my copies, some signed by the players, but as I opened these a host of memories jumped from the pages. There was Dennis 'Bimbo' Hickling, briefly my favourite player because he was from South Yorkshire and so the nearest I had to a hometown player. My dad had underlined some facts in his biography: one of his other hobbies was squash. As I'm sure I did back then, I raised an eyebrow. Bimbo had the build of someone whose idea of exercise was a firm press on the soda siphon, as Sid once said of Cliff Lazarenko. There was also a young Denis Ovens, now the doyen of the darts circuit, still playing, still the source of a million terrible puns ('Ovens' cooking now . . .').

Beneath the pile of programmes was a slim clear plastic folder. I opened it, and the top sheet caught my eye immediately. It was yellow, thick with spider scrawl, but written across the top in readable prose was the word RULES. As always with Sid, there was a date stamp: it was first written in 2005, updated in 2009.

I smiled as I realized these were Sid's rules of commentary. I never knew he had any, though I was aware other commentators did. My first book was published in 1999, a history of BBC TV's cricket coverage written with Stuart Broad's dad, Chris. It was my good fortune to interview a few of my cricketing heroes, including David Gower and Geoff Boycott. Because he was in Australia for their summer, we were unable to interview Richie

Benaud, but he did fax some material over, including his guide to commentary. It made for fascinating reading: 'The *Titanic* was a tragedy, a disaster is a famine in Ethiopia; neither word has a place in cricket commentary' was one. (Richie was the best there's been, but even he failed to live up to his own standard. A day or two after receiving his rules, I was going through some old highlight footage the BBC had sent me of some Test matches from the 1970s. Tony Greig was bowled and Richie said, 'That's a disaster for England . . .')

It has to be said that Sid's commandments differed somewhat from Richie's, but I recount them so future commentators can learn from both men. (Unlike Richie, I'm not sure Sid expected his words to be preserved for future generations, so I have added notes of explanation in italics where necessary to clarify, so their full educational benefit is not lost.)

1. Wake VOICE + fans

Sid was obsessed with his voice, in particular whether it would fail him. Here he's telling himself to make sure his voice was ready when the cue came. Often this would involve him repeating the phrase 'Here we go!' endlessly to himself. As for the fans, my dad's view was that he should get a line in early to get their attention, especially in the initial stages of a tournament when the standard of darts might not be at its most thrilling.

2. APPEARANCE . . .

There were a few things Sid was unable to walk past: a pub, someone seeking an autograph, a shop selling Cornish pasties, and a mirror. But sartorial elegance was often beyond him, so with the help of Irene he built a wardrobe that passed muster (as opposed to one that was mustard – a yellow shirt of his became a pump bag for me at primary school; meanwhile, a red jacket Irene said made him look like a Wallace Arnold coach driver was soon consigned to the charity shop). He was warned off anything bearing a Sky Sports badge. Meanwhile, he shaved every morning because stubble made him look like a tramp. 'Think Vain,' he wrote below. I think this might have been his easiest rule to follow.

3. DRINK – None

Literally, no boozing before commentary. This is one rule my dad rarely broke. On the one occasion he did, heavily and unwisely before a pool match on Sky, he only lasted a few seconds in the box before he was hooked, and he spent the next few weeks in a funk believing that he might be sacked. He never did it again. While the rest of us stood around necking pints before the evening's matches, my dad would sip 'fizzy wattah' in between incantations of 'Here we go!' and prolonged throat clearing. Once he clocked off for the night though, the first pint of 'cooking lager' – his name for anything non-Continental and no stronger than 4 per cent ABV – barely touched the sides.

4. PACE – over week

Sid always tried to rein in his excitement early in the week, with the sensible view that if you screamed like a banshee about a humdrum early-round match, where were you left to go later in the week when the standard improved? His voice, a fragile instrument, also struggled to last if he hammered it too early in the week. See rule 1.

These were the four golden rules, or at least the ones that merited a number. Others followed:

No Swear [*sic*] on TB

My dad recounted with horrified glee other commentators who had said something intemperate down the talkback – the link between the commentary box and the scanner where the director and producer sit – only for it to be broadcast live and their careers ruined. Sid's language was often industrial and profane, so the risks were genuine.

Go to bed + TRY to <u>SLEEP</u> or WALK – or take EX. Gear.

Throughout his life, Sid found sleeping in hotels difficult. A darts tournament is a nocturnal affair. Even when it's played in daytime, inside the venue it feels like night: no natural light, everyone on the beer, spilling into the daylight when the session ends. (It's an enduring irony that the unofficial theme tune for darts, an indoor sport played mostly at night, sung by the whole crowd – Doo-doo-doo-doo doo-dooo-doo dooo-doo-do-doo-doo Oi! Oi! Oi! – at every commercial break is called 'Chase The Sun'.) But daytime sessions are rare, which means the rhythm is unnatural, particularly for a man like my father, who was hardly ever awake at home after 9 p.m. Sometimes his working day wouldn't begin until then. Long days, hectic nights, several hours to wind down, fitful sleep, and then repeat.

Nearly all the players and officials found ways to amuse themselves during the long climb to evening. Mostly this involved golf. Unfortunately, Sid was no golfer. I remember being at a pitch and putt course in childhood, and my dad managed to hit a Land Rover parked at a 90-degree angle to the tee. Once, in Ireland, the tournament sponsors paid for a golf day. Eric Bristow, John Lowe, referee Russ Bray and others resplendent in knitwear each joined different groups of local men, who had paid for the privilege, for a round of golf. Sid, in a cagoule, was asked to join one group. After three holes of watching his incompetent hacking, his group all clocked off and headed for the bar, where in a more familiar habitat he got the Guinness in and entertained them with stories.

In Blackpool, with its seafront and burlesque life, plentiful shops selling rolls and pasties, he was fine. But in places like Purfleet, in Identikit hotels stuck beside featureless dual carriageways and ring roads, he was left with no option but to yomp Alan Partridge-like to the local garage for snacks. It drove him crazy. Much of his commentary was an outburst of pent-up energy after being coiled during the day, scouring his notes, watching the clock tick by slowly until it was time to explode.

His one other release was a game of pool. He would drag poor Dave Lanning along to the worst dives he could find, the tattier and more threadbare the better: 'upholstered sewers' he would call them. One time in Vegas, acting on a tip, he and Dave took a cab to a place called Pool Sharks, ten miles out in the desert where even coyotes feared to roam. But he was welcomed like a homecoming hero. When the time came to return to the MGM Grand for some darts, they were told no taxi would collect them from that part of town. A man with a van agreed to give them a lift, but as his snarling dog refused to let them in beside it, they sat sweltering in the back with a cargo of mini totem poles and other Native American knick-knacks, clinging on for dear life. As ever, the tale made its way into their next commentary together, with Dave corpsing Sid with a reference to 'Big Chief Hitting Bull'.

As for exercise gear, well, I never saw Sid in a gym in my life. In a moment of madness, he and Irene bought a Nordic ski machine. Occasionally, my dad would come downstairs and boast that he'd done a kilometre. I'd try to point out that in an alpine resort that would hardly get you from chalet to ski lift, but for him it was an *achievement. His only other exercise was to pick up a kitchen chair and lift it five times with each hand. I still don't know why.*

The rest of the sheet is filled with short phrases the meaning of which, even to me, is not often clear. 'Comm Crossfire . . . look at oppo' reads one, which I presume is a warning not to talk at the same time as his co-commentator and to anticipate when his partner was going to speak. 'Ritual – do not break' is more cryptic, as it does not specify what the ritual is. 'Cut Alc Coffee Cheese' is self-explanatory but another that often went unheeded. In large capitals, Irene has written 'YOU ARE ALLERGIC'. This is another reference to alcohol, which in excessive quantities made my dad cough and spit the next day; red wine gave him gout and spirits made him vomit. Hence the reliance on humble 'cooking lager' as his social lubricant at the darts.

I doubt Richie Benaud had to write the same self-admonishments.

The Power

THE GREAT DARTS WAR is now over. The PDC stand victorious. Their 'brand' sells out arenas designed to host stadium-swallowing rock bands, they have the best players in the world under their banner and quickly attract the best newcomers from across the divide who see a chance to make money on the professional circuit. The BDO continues to do a fine job promoting amateur darts, but its professional game is lacklustre. The Embassy is now the Lakeside, kept afloat only by Bob Potter's largesse and some half-hearted BBC TV coverage. It's a dated, muted relic of the vibrant, raucous tournament it once was. The BDO try to offer their professionals and top-end players tournaments and opportunities to earn and compete, but even they know the game is up and that the flow of talent to the PDC is a tide that can't be turned. There is even talk of the unthinkable: darting glasnost, a rapprochement between the two organizations. If only Sid and others were alive to see it happen.

But for a number of years after the split and beyond, the issue of which code was the strongest and which World Championship was best was a source of passionate debate among darts and sport fans. In those first WDC Worlds, there is no doubt they had the finer, more talented top eight, most of whom would have been seeded in a unified game. But where the BDO had the edge was in depth of talent: players who had qualified for the Embassy and were excellent performers in county and international darts, who made the tournament tougher than the WDC equivalent for the higher seeds. New faces like Richie Burnett, Les Wallace, Mervyn King and notably Raymond van Barneveld were given the chance to get used to the stage. And of course, because of the ban, the BDO had first dibs on the best international players. Though no fault of their own, the WDC had to rely on American players, and at times their tournament had an Anglo-American feel to it.

As the form of the WDC's old guard started to fade, and there was no opportunity for younger players to come through and replace them other than those brave enough to risk calumny and isolation, there was an argument that the BDO's World Championship was of a higher standard. But it was brief, and even then the old guard were still able to turn in vintage perormances: first John Lowe when he pushed Phil Taylor all the way in the 1995 semi-final, and even more memorably when Eric Bristow cast off his dartitis, as if healed by a higher power, to scare the living daylights out of Taylor in the 1997 semi and produce an epic encounter, which Sid enjoyed for its subtext and allegorical potential. 'Merlin never gave Arthur a bashing like this,' he screamed, voice breaking, as Bristow threatened to topple his protégé, the man whose phenomenal talent he had first nurtured and sponsored. 'What's the melting point of microphone metal?'

Taylor overcame Eric's last hurrah and went on to claim his

fifth World Championship by beating Dennis Priestley with a three-dart average of more than 100. At the time, it seemed momentous, but it marked the start of an unbelievable spell of dominance where he raised darts to a level no one thought possible. 'They won't just have to play outta their skin to beat Phil Taylor. They'll have to play outta their essence!' as Sid said. Whichever new players or champions the BDO tournament threw up in those years, the PDC always had Taylor and therefore the world's best player. Any other darts player who even wished to be considered the best had no option but to cross the divide and challenge the greatest or forever live in his shadow.

As Taylor started to dominate the game like no other man had done before, or is likely to in the future, Sid revelled in his brilliance. He felt proud and privileged to chronicle his breathtaking achievements and was mesmerized by his ability to improve even when no one was able to touch him. 'Look at the man go: it's like trying to stop a water buffalo with a pea-shooter!'

Sky were equally enamoured with Taylor. Viewing figures were always highest when he was playing, so his matches attracted the hype and were scheduled at peak time, and Sid was always asked to commentate on them. This led to some criticism from darts fanatics that Sid and Sky were too much in thrall to the Power and too over-enthusiastic in their praise. Sid dismissed this as nonsense: he knew darts fans were lucky to be alive in the time of Taylor and offered no apology for pointing out his sustained brilliance. 'The bloke's a genius, and there's no point hiding it,' he told me. 'The trick is to match the words to his genius.'

Taylor also gave Sid something he had always wanted: a chance to commentate on a nine-dart finish. They are almost commonplace now, but at one point it was the darting Holy Grail. Sid was visibly jealous when John Lowe produced the first televised nine-dart on ITV in 1984, so handing Dave Lanning the honour of being the first to commentate on it. He was even more envious when he learned that Dave had placed a bet on a player to do it that year at odds of 250–1 and had trousered almost as much as Lowe.

But that resentment was nothing compared to the pang he felt in 1989 when Paul Lim performed the second televised perfect leg during the Embassy *and Tony Green was commentating*. I spoke to him on the phone and he was *malade comme un perroquet*, to quote a commentary of his from the same year.

He yearned for one, and after he switched to Sky and Taylor's form reached for it, it seemed as if it might happen in every tournament. 'Please let me be on comms when it does,' he prayed.

I was in a pub in Ealing when it did, the darts on a muted TV in the background. Taylor was playing Chris Mason in the quarter-finals of the World Matchplay in Blackpool, and I was only half paying attention. I heard a gasp from across the empty pub: Taylor had hit back-to-back 180s and the nine-dart was on. But the sound was off, and the bemused Polish woman behind the bar had no idea how to turn it up. So I had to watch Sid's finest moment without Sid's voice. He called me after the match, bubbling with excitement. Dave Lanning, beside him as it happened, had done it again: placed a bet on it happening and won them both some money. He asked if I'd seen it, and I said I had. He asked what I thought of his commentary, and I lied and said it was brilliant, though I'd not heard a word. (Sid had actually screeched 'History! History! History!' so loud and in such a high pitch as Taylor landed double 12 that he was heard by several dogs in Fleetwood.)

~

He and Phil were friends, though not especially close. Taylor is a singular man, which is part of the reason for his success. Not for him late nights at the bar, beer with the boys or tall tales and shaggy-dog stories. He rested and practised incessantly, changing his darts and challenging himself constantly to improve. Sid admired his single-mindedness and discipline.

He ghostwrote Taylor's autobiography and spent several sessions interviewing him. One took place in the back room in Pudsey, looking out into the garden. Sid was trying to coax the Power into recalling his feelings over the loss earlier that year of his world crown to the Canadian John Part, after a monumental tussle that would stand as the greatest game of them all until Taylor's defeat to van Barneveld four years later. 'How did it feel,' asked Sid, voice hushed, 'to lose your title? Here was Part, a man who had crossed the Rubicon to come and try to beat you. Whom you defeated, nay crushed into powder, in the 2001 final, but who now gained his revenge and thus achieved his dream, taking away from you what you treasured most? How crushing was that disappointment?'

Taylor paused, gazing into the middle distance. In Sid's mind, he was reliving every dart of the harrowing final set, when Part ended his run of eight consecutive titles, drinking in the smoke and tears and disappointment. His eyes narrowed. Eventually, he spoke.

'Sid,' he said. 'Who fitted your French windows?'

'What?' my dad responded.

Taylor rose from his chair and started to fiddle with the window. He asked for a screwdriver. Sid fetched one. Taylor fiddled around for a few seconds more. 'There you go,' he said. 'Sorted.'

He sat back down. 'Where were we?'

'John Part. This year's final.'

'Ah yes,' Taylor said. 'I'll beat him next time.'

The book was released in 2004. Shortly after its launch, Sid asked him what he reckoned of it. How did it feel to have his life laid out in print? What did he think of Sid's efforts to do justice to his towering achievements?

'I haven't read it,' he said. 'I looked at the photos though. Why did you use one that made me look really fat?'

My dad was gobsmacked. Sid was a man who would cross the Arctic tundra in his underpants just to read a downpage news in brief in the *Daily Star* that *might* mention his name. Yet here was man who had had a book written about his life but had not read a word of it. 'The bloke doesn't do self-analysis or reflection,' he told me afterwards. 'The bloke does darts and winning. That's the Power, kid.'

Voice of the Balls

A s the twentieth century drew to a close, there was a brief thaw in the darts Cold War. There were still two World Championships, but with the court case settled and the ban lifted, for a brief period PDC players played in BDO Opens, while the BDO players took the chance to take a potshot at Taylor. There were those who argued that having two codes diluted the sport, confused the viewers and was bad for the game. I don't think that was the case. Having one tournament a year on the BBC, even denuded of the world's finest players, kept the sport in the public eye during those years when the PDC was putting down roots and dreaming up schemes and grand plans. The BDO and Lakeside also acted as an unwitting preparatory school for the PDC, producing the finest talent, putting them on stage and thus allowing the PDC to identify who they did and didn't want to poach.

The stream of BDO defectors reinvigorated the PDC, alongside a growing number of tournaments on Sky. Gradually, in the public mind it became the better-known and the better code. Much credit for this must go to Barry Hearn, the promoter more famous as a snooker impresario during that sport's 1980s golden age. The way Sid told the story, Hearn turned up at a PDC tournament in the late 1990s and surveyed the baying crowd and throbbing atmosphere. 'I smell money,' he said.

Battle-hardened but wearied from their legal war with the BDO, Dick Allix and Tommy Cox were looking for someone to complete the sport's revival. Hearn was that man: he negotiated new TV deals, worked hard to bring in new, illustrious sponsors, enticed the best players from what he called 'the Dark Side' and took darts beyond the UK and Europe. This included a tournament in Las Vegas that in order to be screened at prime time in the UK needed to be played at lunchtime in the US. It proved a challenge for the organizers to round up those players – and the odd commentator – who had found the varied attractions of Vegas too tempting to have an early night, or indeed any kind of night. It was not unknown for certain people to be plucked straight from the roulette table and marched to the practice room or stage.

The sport's growing profile brought more publicity, which invariably centred on Taylor and Sid. This meant more work for Sid, not all of it successful. In 1999, Chris Evans was commissioned to make a prime-time Saturday evening programme called *Red Alert*. It would feature the draw for the National Lottery, whose voice since its inception had been Alan Dedicoat. Someone came up with the wheeze of getting Sid to do it. Initially, he was reluctant – until he saw the cheque; then he was persuaded. He ventured down to London to make the first episode. It was filmed live, and it was a disaster. Sid sounded nervous and barely comprehensible. But he may still have been the best part of the programme, which was a rambling, incoherent mess. It was panned by the critics, and complaints poured in about the weird Geordie bloke who was the voice of the balls.

Sid was sacked but still paid for a full series: an ideal result given how universally derided the programme was until put out of its misery. He even managed to turn the shambles to his own advantage by planting a story in the press, run eagerly by many, that he was sacked because of his Geordie accent and not because his voice didn't fit. He was probably the only person to emerge from the sorry saga with his reputation intact.

Sky also employed his talents in other sports, including pool, which was ideal given his love of the game. He was a far better pool player than darts, and played three or four times a week. His commentary suited the sport perfectly, and it highlighted some memorable characters, especially crowd-baiting, mulleted, unhinged US bad boy Earl 'the Pearl' Strickland and former snooker champion Steve Davis, rechristened Romford Slim by Sid for his new venture. It revived some of the old *Indoor League* spirit in Sid, as did some of the venues. 'Oh, and would you see the look of denouement on the face of Romford Slim here at the Goresbrook Leisure Centre!' he once screamed, a public baths bringing out his bathetic best. And another: 'You can tug on Superman's cape, you can spit into the wind, you can pull the mask off the old Lone Ranger but DON'T MESS AROUND WITH ROMFORD SLIM!'

(Thanks to the *Independent*'s Tom Peck for reminding me of that first line, as well as another Sid quote wherein he describes the reasons behind his vivid attack on the patter, aka his shouting. 'It's not like Marcel Proust,' he said of his commentaries. 'You can't muse for forty pages about the bottom of a digestive biscuit.' Tom also remembers working at the Lakeside – no, not that one, but a mega-mall in Thurrock, Essex – and stumbling across the pool being filmed there. Earl the Pearl had won and was telling his interlocutor, in his southern drawl, 'Thank God, I wanna THANK GOD, for letting us play here today. Lakeside, you are incredible.' I remember Sid telling me there had been a second take of one player's walk-on, which involved exiting the glass lift near Claire's Accessories to the music of the New Radicals, because the first time he emerged he was accompanied by an old lady in a mac pulling a wheelie shopping trolley . . .)

Occasionally, the atmosphere at the pool threatened to overheat; once, at Goresbrook, the referee had to warn the crowd about their rowdiness. 'No one wants to see the fair name of Dagenham smudged by ungentlemanly behaviour,' said Sid.

Less suited to Sid's milieu was ten-pin bowling, for which his research was having watched Woody Harrelson mistakenly drink bull semen in *Kingpin*. He and I did spend some time at the Merrion Bowl in Leeds preparing for his commentaries, but after he shot 38 and stuck seven out of twenty bowls in the gutter, we decided the time would be better invested in the Whitelock's, drinking pints of William Younger's No. 3.

Yet that was still more research than he managed for his most bizarre televised commentary outing: clay pigeon shooting. 'I finally get to commentate on an outdoor sport and it involves farmers in wellies and Barbours with guns,' he moaned. Even though he knew as much about it as he did lacrosse, he was, according to Dave Lee, the young producer tasked with turning it into something watchable, a complete professional. 'My favourite bits were making up the daft intros with Sid. We'd just stick him in a situation and he'd improvise something. He made one up once comparing himself to Churchill, can't remember how it went, but it was ace.'

Unfortunately, at least in the case of the pool, Sid had to leave these extracurricular activities behind as more and more tournaments were added to the darts roster. He missed the pool and the camaraderie he shared with Jim Wych and Steve Davis. 'It's probably just as well, kidda,' he told me with a grin. 'Soon they'd have had us commentating on dwarf tossing!'

A Bit of Fry and Waddell

WITH THE PDC unstoppable in the 2000s, Sid sat back and enjoyed the ride. There were so many great matches, so much excellence from Taylor, and the arrival of young pretenders to his throne, that he was never short of dramatic material with which to work. By now, it was a performance.

There were the odd kinks, namely when he lost his voice during the 2003 World Championship and had to be taken off the final, to his disgust. To prevent it happening again, he consulted a voice coach, who told him that his hunched posture at the microphone caused tension in his upper body, and that he had a tendency to screech ('No shit,' said millions of darts fans), which was ravaging his vocal cords. But he encouraged Sid to open up his chest, relax and gargle with salt water. He also suggested he prepare with breathing and vocal exercises that sounded like the mating call of a whale who'd not had it in months. Sid would perform these exercises for anyone who would care to listen, which after a few months was nobody. But he credited them with prolonging both his voice and commentary career.

He had also, in Dave Lanning's words, become 'bigger than

the business'. Taylor aside, there was by now no more well-known person in the game. This presented its problems. Sid had always enjoyed mingling and mixing with the fans, signing autographs, posing for photographs and chatting away to even the drunkest skunk. But darts had risen to such a level of popularity, and was being played in front of so many people, that each time he ventured beyond the security barriers that separated players and officials from the great unwashed, he was mobbed. The tipping point came during a Premier League night in Newcastle, where a horde descended on him in good nature, but by the end his shirt was ripped and someone had inadvertently punched him in the nuts. From then on, for his own safety, he arrived and left through the stage door and steered clear of the masses.

He joined the modern world when Irene ordered him to get a mobile phone, albeit against his will. Until then he had been the last of the bohemians: he didn't drive, couldn't work a computer, and used cash not credit cards. He was very much an analogue man in the digital world, who preferred the backstreet to the high street. Irene insisted he got a mobile phone, and it baffled him.

'What are them symbols?' he asked me once, thrusting it towards me.

'It means you've got voice messages,' I said.

I checked: he had more than fifty voicemails; none of them had been listened to.

But voice and voice messages aside, mainly it was gravy, culminating in Stephen Fry's appearance alongside Sid in the commentary box for the Premier League finals of 2010. The Prem, as it was known, had become the sport's biggest cash cow. When it started in 2005, it was a round-robin competition that played to reasonable crowds at leisure centres in Widnes and Doncaster. Three years later, it was selling out Wembley Arena. I remember seeing Dick Allix and Tommy Cox sipping champagne in the bar at Wembley, reflecting how far they and the sport had come from the Talk nightclub in Norwich in 1992, and the sacrifices and struggles since, and here they were at the home of British sport. By 2010, darts was played every single week at vast arenas across the United Kingdom.

Before the 2010 finals night, sharp-witted Sky sports PR man James Motley had the idea to ask Fry along. He regularly tweeted his love of darts to his million plus followers, and as the sport now attracted royalty in its VIP section, why not ask one of Britain's most treasured comic actors along and grab an interview? Fry agreed and turned up at Wembley Arena, only for a power cut to plunge the venue into darkness. The darts was postponed till the next night. Could Fry make it back? He wasn't sure. He was supposed to be at a 'serious dinner' hosted by royalty, but this was too good a chance to miss. Prince Charles could wait, Sid and the Power couldn't.

He had also agreed to join Sid and ex-pro Rod Harrington in the commentary box for the semi-final between Phil Taylor and Mervyn King. I spoke to Sid on the phone during the day. He said Fry was going to commentate with him. I felt a flutter of apprehension in my stomach. First, I was unsure whether Sid knew exactly who Fry was. He didn't watch TV. He certainly knew *of* him, but did he appreciate what he had done? Second, guest turns in the commentary box often turned into stumbling exercises in fawning: a sort of semi-interview, 'How's your new book?' cringe.

Fry observed Sid's pent-up act prior to kick-off. He told me: 'Before the match he had been nervous, his brow creased, and he paced up and down and scribbled wildly on to a notepad. I realized this was the professional in him, cramming in all the stats and all the history between the two players who were coming on to the oche. So many details, most of which would never need to be mentioned, but he was never ever under-primed.'

But as soon as they were sitting in the commentary box, Sid relaxed. 'I felt as if I was in a dream. Crammed into that hot, tiny space with Sid nudging and battering me with his hands and elbows and delighting me with his impish grins and wild twitches.'

I need not have worried. It worked brilliantly. Sid dived deep and emerged with a pearl to begin with when he introduced the commentary trio for the evening: 'Sid Waddell, BA Cantab, Stephen Fry, BA Cantab, Rodney Harrington, University of Life.' From then on it flowed. A camera on the box proved as compelling as the footage on stage, Sid subjecting Fry to the tics and flicks anyone who knew him and had sat next to him knew so well: a friendly physical assault of nudges and pushes. Fry entered into the spirit with his own lyrical turn. 'I'm as happy as a pig in Chardonnay,' he said.

The match ended with Taylor rampant. 'Once upon a time he was breaking all records, now he's only breaking all hearts. Nothing you can do, total eclipse of the dart.'

'Ah, Bonnie Taylor,' sighed Fry.

It had been an unlikely yet beautiful meeting of minds. I asked Sid later what he thought.

'We had a bloody ball.'

The Healing Power of Darts

I N THE SUMMER of 2011, Sid started to experience some stomach pain and discomfort. He told me about a helicopter ride in which he and Eric Bristow flew from the Matchplay in Blackpool to York races for a sponsored event, where his intestinal turmoil was such that he forgot to be scared of crashing. But as it came and went, he put it down to a persistent stomach bug. In truth, he'd not felt well all year: after the 2011 World Championship, he'd had an infection, lost weight and needed to go on antibiotics. Perhaps the stomach pain was a result of those drugs?

He eventually went to the doctor. Within two weeks, he was referred to the hospital for tests and scans. It soon became clear it was serious and that there was an obstruction in his bowel. I feared the worst and others did too. But nothing prepared us for how bad it was. It was bowel cancer, it was at an advanced stage, and it was inoperable.

Sid did not suit illness and vice versa. No one does really, but there are stoics who can bear the burden of serious illness, meditate on mortality and suffering, and retain their equilibrium. But Sid was no stoic: he was a hypochondriac and psychosomatic. So much as sneeze near him and he contracted a cold. God forbid if someone vomited: he'd be hanging over the bowl in anticipation. The irony was that, despite his cough, his chest and asthma, he was never seriously ill in his life. He was in good nick for a man of his age and always looked younger than his years.

He was also maudlin and scared of death. Again, who isn't? But Sid seemed offended by the idea of his own mortality. In his days as a serious boozer, he used to tell Irene he wouldn't see forty. Then it was forty-five. Then it was fifty, until he was into middle age and dying young was no longer an option. The healthy, clean-living father of my first serious girlfriend succumbed to cancer when he was in his forties. She and her family were distraught, and I spent much of my eighteenth year comforting her as his condition worsened, or trying to at least, returning home late at night exhausted and spent. Sid would be up waiting for me, sometimes with drink taken, brow furrowed and a sombre tone in his voice. He wanted to talk about it. But not because it felt like he was trying to ease my burden, though that might well have been his intention, but because Joanne's dad was around the same age as him, and he couldn't help but put himself in his shoes and contemplate his own death.

Whenever someone he knew died, even a long-lost friend or distant relative, he would descend into melancholy. It irritated me, to be honest, as if he was wallowing in it, using it as an excuse for self-pity rather than sympathizing with those who had lost someone they had loved. It was never: 'My God, they've died, how sad.' It was: 'My God, I'll die, how horrific.'

But, like it does to all of us, the death of his parents toughened him up, as did the untimely end of Derrick and then the tragic sudden death of his nephew Robbie.

Then, in 2003, my first wife Emma was diagnosed with breast cancer six months after the birth of our son. The week before, the hospital had given her the all-clear. We spilled out into the September sunshine and headed for lunch, where we drank champagne and sloughed off the awful anxiety of the previous few weeks. A week later, we were summoned back. There had been a mistake; she had cancer. We stumbled out into the same soft autumn sunshine, but now our world had changed.

Sid and Irene were brilliant. The week after the diagnosis we went on a planned holiday with them to Sitges in Spain. It turned out it was the gay capital of Spain, but that didn't throw Sid; he even contemplated buying a muscle vest ('Can I buy some muscles first?'). I feared he would be maudlin, but he was upbeat and supportive, and we had a wonderful, regenerative week.

Emma had treatment and recovered. The prognosis was good. But in the summer of 2005, the cancer returned, and this time there was no chance of recovery. It had spread to her brain, and she became extremely sick. Our son Dougie could not comprehend what was happening. The dying resemble people drifting out to sea. Every now and then a wave brings them closer to shore and you catch a fleeting, cruel glimpse of their old self and convince yourself they are improving. The next time you look, they have been washed further away, distant and lost. Dougie, quite naturally, though I know it broke his mother's heart, uncoupled himself from her and attached himself to me.

Sid and Irene again stepped in. If Sid was an unconventional dad, he made for a more orthodox grandfather. If he parented at arms' length, his grandfathering was hands-on. We broke arms, smashed cheekbones, gashed limbs and were barely a week out of Casualty. Sid was there with a consoling hug, but he was hardly warding off trouble. But as a grandparent he became concerned and wary, warning children of the pitfalls and pratfalls attached to their actions. It was as if he had finally woken up to the fact that the world could be a dangerous place.

Some things didn't change though. When my fearless nephew Bobby climbed to the top of an intricate rope tower in Pudsey park, Sid was horrified he would fall. 'Go and get him down,' he said – to Irene, then sixty-four, with two arthritic knees. Bobby once became stuck in a funfair funhouse and jammed the wobbling floor in the process. Sid went in to get him out. It was a toss-up to determine which attracted most complaints from other kids and parents: the snot-nosed kid that broke the ride or the old man screaming out 'Shit!' and 'Fuck!' every five seconds as he wobbled through the Shake Shack, waded through the ball pool, went headfirst through a foam mangle and banged his head twenty times in a maze of mirrors to rescue his grandson.

Grandparenting suited him better: the silly songs and phrases delighted all his grandkids. (Dougie and my stepdaughter Maya, ubercool teenagers now, still sing his Toast song: 'Toasty toast is very nice / You have it once, you have it twice / Tell your friends out at the coast / We all love toasty toast.') The way they mangled words amused him, while he'd happily sit and watch children's TV for hours on end, often weaving references even more arcane than his allusions to nineteenth-century French playwrights into his commentary. 'He's not yella, he's not got big red spots, but Lloydy is a ferocious beast,' I once heard him saying, a reference that only those members of his audience who happened to watch Nickelodeon Junior on weekdays at 7.30 p.m. between 2005 and 2008 might understand.

Throughout Emma's endless hospital trips and stays, and emergencies and scares, they travelled up and down from Leeds to London to care for Dougie and support me and Emma. Then, on a bleak March day of grey skies and pouring rain, they were in the room with me and her family when Emma died. She was thirty-seven.

It changed me, it changed all of us, and it changed Sid. In those last few bewildering days of Emma's life, he told me how Derrick had accused him of never being around when there was illness or death. It seemed unfair. When he learned of his uncle Sam's death, he was filming in East Anglia and immediately hired a taxi to drive him more than two hundred miles to the North. But the words had stung, and he was determined to bear witness to his daughter-in-law's death, even though I could see how difficult it was for him. But he knew I needed him there. In the last few hours of her life, Emma demanded we drink champagne. Sid left the hospice to buy a bottle. The only place he could find it was a corner shop. It was warm. He wasn't having that, so he laid the bottle in a deep, freezing puddle and stood on Ladbroke Grove in the pissing rain for half an hour until it had chilled.

In the days and months that followed, Sid and Irene helped me and Dougie rebuild our lives. The offer was there to move back to Pudsey and the sanctuary of the large house on South Parade they had bought in 1982 and lived in ever since. It acted as a refuge for us all: no matter what crisis we faced, what vagaries life threw at us, South Parade was always there, with Irene to listen and advise, while Sid cracked open the wine and cracked the jokes. Splits, divorces, job losses, deaths, vulnerability – we all ran for home as fast as we could. There would be no judging, no opinions, simply pure support. When Lucy's marriage ended, Sid was at the door to meet her and give her a hug: 'You can't live your life at sixty kilowatts when you're a hundred kilowatts person,' he told her, words that applied to himself. He knew. We joked about how unpractical he was, mocked his technophobia and how over-emotional he could be, but he knew people and he knew life's vicissitudes; he had made his mistakes and had his share of the breaks, and he knew how to pull through.

I had Googled his cancer and its stage; I knew there was no chance of a recovery. But when I went to see him in October 2011, shortly after he started treatment to prolong his life, I was encouraged. He was philosophical and calm. He seemed more worried for the rest of us. 'You realize when you reach my age it's not just about you,' he told me. He also looked back on his career. 'I've been lucky. I ended up being good at something I never knew I'd be good at.'

Darts hadn't saved him, but it had made him. In 1978, he was treading water as a TV producer, after a turbulent period of his life both professionally and privately. There had been only fleeting success as a scriptwriter and failure as a novelist and it looked as if his desire to make a mark on the world would be thwarted. But then came darts – and the rest was history.

How much commentary had come to mean to him was clear that week in Pudsey. The World Grand Prix in Dublin was on, but after his diagnosis Sid had pulled out. It suddenly felt unimportant, and he told me over the phone he probably wouldn't commentate again, whatever happened. He didn't want people asking after his health and having to put a brave face on a diagnosis of terminal cancer. So he withheld the truth of its seriousness, said he would take some time off but would be back, even if he wasn't sure whether that would happen.

But the treatment wasn't bad initially, and he felt better. We sat and watched the darts, and I could tell he wanted to be there. He gasped with delight every time a good dart hit the board, winced when he thought the commentary was lacklustre or a comment didn't fit. I half expected him to pick up his beer bottle as a mic and start using it. We both knew he could have and should have gone. The next week he called me to say he'd been in touch with Sky, and he was going to be at the World Championship for a few days; I could sense the excitement in his voice.

Sid was back.

The Death of a Patriarch

Shortly before Christmas, an adverse reaction to a bout of chemo wiped Sid out, and he never made it to the Alexandra Palace. It sparked decline: in the New Year he lost weight, the drugs stopped working and made him worse, the pain increased and his mood darkened. The faint glimmer of hope that he would respond miraculously well to the treatment dimmed.

Unbelievably, given his condition, he did make it to a few Premier League nights to commentate. I was there in early April when a car was due to collect and take him from Pudsey to the Capital FM Arena in Nottingham at 3 p.m. to commentate on the first match and then bring him back straight after. He didn't get out of bed until late morning, came down the stairs in great discomfort, grumbled as he chewed on some toast and took enough pills to fill a pharmacy. Then he sat half-asleep in an armchair, wincing in pain, crying out when he got up. I left before he did, but I spoke to Irene and wondered if it was wise to let him go in that state. She said the shot of adrenaline he got behind the mic helped take his focus away from the pain. 'He'll be fine,' she reassured me.

With some trepidation, I switched on that evening. But Irene, as ever, had been right. There was a brittle quality to his voice that matched his now brittle physique, and it wasn't his best commentary by any means, but he was still definitely Sid, and it was clear that the unrecognizable pained old man of that morning had been replaced by a more vivacious, familiar person. The darts, the lights, the commentary box, his mates and 'the smell of the tungsten and the sound of the crowd' had worked an effect no drug could and made him forget he was dying. For a brief period, he was doing something he truly loved; everything else, in his words, 'could gan and pelt shite'.

It was difficult not to picture him sitting in the back of the car on the way home, gazing out of the window as the aches and pain crept back and so did the reality, wondering if he would get another chance.

He did: seven more appearances at venues close enough for Irene to drive him there and back in a day. The exception was Glasgow, another dirty city that Sid loved, where they made a short holiday of it, staying in an upmarket hotel in the city centre. The doorman welcomed him like an old friend. Sid realized he was: it was someone he had met while working on the Matchplay in Blackpool. The man had never forgotten how Sid had taken time to talk to him and his wife. The affection shown to Sid by this man alone made the trip worthwhile.

His last commentary was the semi-final at the 0_2 Arena in London on 17 May 2012, between James Wade and, fittingly, Phil Taylor. For this, he and Irene had to make the journey down by train, but Sky laid on a car to ferry him around London. In two months, his condition had worsened further, but he still refused to miss it. His performance doesn't really matter; in the circumstances it's a miracle he's there, but he does all right. His chemo-fogged brain means fewer one-liners and allusions, but he still manages to rise to the occasion. 'I've learned more being here with you, Sidney, than I have in my previous thirty-seven years on this planet,' his co-commentator Wayne Mardle says. 'I thought you said you were thirty-nine last week,' replied Sid. There was a light, and it hadn't gone out. The game and Sid's career ended in suitably familiar fashion. Taylor hits 'fat 20' to leave double top, which he hits, as Sid cries 'Lipstick!'

In July, he and Irene moved from Pudsey to Harrogate. Within two weeks, he was in a hospice to try to control his medication, as the pain was worsening and he was increasingly agitated. I went up to see him; he was back on the steroids and seemed in good spirits, if sometimes snappy and wired from the drugs in his veins. He was barely eating. He talked ten to the dozen: Sid was one man who didn't need steroids. The World Matchplay had started in Blackpool. He had been oblivious. We gave him an iPad to watch it on, and my brother-in-law Richard had to drive back and forth all evening acting as technical support because he didn't know how to use it and kept switching it off accidentally. But once again the restorative power of darts had worked its magic – the next day one of my other brothers-in-law, Simon, even discussed taking him to Blackpool on the back of his motorbike to commentate for a match. Simon was joking; Sid was serious.

I went back to London, heart heavy. In between the jokes and darts, he had also been agitated and ratty. I could tell that once the steroids wore off, he would slump, and I wanted to be there to speak to him and try to ease his anxiety. I didn't want to leave. But I had a family in London who needed me. I left for the train in the rain, hoping there was still some life in the old dog.

～

Irene called on Friday, 3 August. 'It's time to come up,' she said. Early the next morning, I took a train from London to York and changed on to the rattler to Harrogate. My eldest sister Lucy picked me up from the station, her face drawn and tight. She drove me to Irene and Sid's new flat.

Sid had come home from the hospice, and his condition had deteriorated. As I walked in, I sensed a familiar odour, one I'd experienced six years earlier and never wanted to smell again.

He was in bed, eyes closed. His eyes were sunken, his cheeks hollow, and his skin had a grey, translucent quality. It was as if someone had drained him of all the energy and vivacity that made him Sid, and the man on the bed was a pallid ghost. There was a chair beside the bed. I sat down and took his hand in mine. It was cold and clammy but delicate. We had always joked between us that neither had done a proper's day work in our lives and had the soft silky hands to show for it.

His eyes flickered and opened. He turned and saw me and smiled weakly.

'All right, Dad.'

His eyes closed again. 'All right, kid.'

I gave his hand a squeeze. He drifted into unconsciousness. When he did surface, he was semi-lucid. As cancer takes its final, fatal grip, the sufferer starts to hallucinate, to see things that aren't there, often faces or people from the past. I couldn't make out what he was saying, and as soon as he spoke his eyes closed and he was gone again. Drifting further away from the shore.

That evening, with no one else there, I sat beside him again. The window was open, and a wind billowed the curtains. It started to rain, and its soft susurration added an ambient calm. It was still light, but inside with the curtains closed and no light it was womblike. His breathing was slow and steady. I held his hand again and his eyes opened. He half turned towards me and smiled. This time his eyes remained open.

'Where are they?'

His voice was a hoarse, dry whisper. I picked up a glass of water and helped him take a sip.

Everyone was out grabbing food. I was going to join them later, and Irene would come back to replace me at his bedside. But I wanted to spend as much time here as I could. This might be the last time we ever spoke. Tears started to stream down my cheeks, but it was too dark for him to see.

'They're having a bite to eat. They'll be back in a bit.'

I felt his hand squeeze mine. I think he knew from my voice I was crying.

He turned again, this time to face me. This was not how he wanted it to be, wasting away like this in front of us.

'We had some laughs, didn't we?'

I let out a snotty, teary laugh.

'Did we ever,' I said, using one of his favourite phrases.

The corners of his mouth turned up in a smile, then his eyes closed, and he sank back into unconsciousness.

～

Nick arrived, my sister Emma too, to join Charlotte and Lucy, who already lived in Harrogate. Each day we sat in the sitting room drinking tea and wine, taking it in turns to maintain a vigil beside his bed. The London Olympics were on, and we would move from one room where this great pageant was being screened, to another to sit beside our father as he shuffled slowly out of life. Irene pointed out it would make the backdrop to a great play, one that Sid would almost certainly have appreciated. The death of the patriarch: the joy and celebration of life in one room; the sombre slide into death in another.

Irene's sister Sheila, her brother-in-law John, niece Becky and great-niece Emma arrived in Harrogate. The year before, plans had been made for them to come over from their home in the US to go to the Olympics. Irene had joined the lottery for tickets and managed to snag diving, and archery at Lord's. They had attended those events without Irene and Sid, but it wasn't the same. Now they found themselves saying goodbye to a much-loved member of their family.

From the middle of the week, Sid was unconscious. By Thursday, our vigils were running through the night. Friday was his seventy-second birthday.

On Saturday evening, with us all sitting around him, he died.

The undertaker arrived shortly before midnight.

'Pleased to meet you,' I said at the door.

'No, you're not,' he said immediately.

Sharp Northern humour shot through with black mordant wit. Somewhere, Sid laughed appreciatively.

Valhalla

ONE WARM AUGUST morning in 2015, I walked around Lynemouth. I started at the Hot L, now no longer a pub; the main bar where my uncle Derrick pickled his liver is now a café serving artery-furring 'Bellybusta' breakfasts, while the other half is a library and resource centre, which my dad opened a decade or so ago. The green fields and dogshit of the Welfare are now covered with new houses, while the garage where my auntie Gladys worked has gone, replaced with a fishing tackle shop. Other casualties include the Pakistani shop, the Co-op, the butcher's, even the church where my grandmother dragged me with her on a Sunday night. One evening, she spent the entire service looking at me from the corner of her eye, her thirty-a-day laugh rumbling, and I wondered what I had done. Afterwards, barely able to speak between wheezy giggles, she told me she thought I had taken money from the collection plate when it came round, rather than handing over the pound note she had given to me to donate. I hadn't, but Martha was Sid's mum, and the refusal to let a good anecdote slip through the fingers was obviously a Smith trait, so it was retold, always with a mischievous twinkle in her eye, as if stealing from the Lord was in some way admirable.

The Tute is still there, though it was closed that morning. I cupped my hands to either side of my forehead to block out the light of the sun and peered through the window, noting the lack of a snooker table. But at least old miners still have somewhere to drink. Other survivors include the Chinese, still trying to sell us egg foo yung, and the chip shop. I walked on to Dalton Avenue, past the newly rebuilt school, towards 102. As I got closer, the cloying late-summer smell of privet flowers gave way to a more familiar scent – smoke. Not as thick or as acrid as it once was, but still there – the heady smell of Lynemouth sea coal. I glanced around the chimney tops, trying to see the tell-tale dark swirls of smoke, but there were none. Who would be burning a fire on such a glorious day anyway?

I reached 102. It was unrecognizable: the front part of the garden had been paved over to build a parking bay; the section nearest the house, where my grandfather had grown his leeks and potatoes, was now covered with a lean-to conservatory. Around the back, the coal hole was filled in and painted over; the cree and netty had both been demolished to make way for an extension. Back here, the smell of smoke had gone, but as I walked back around to the front it returned. Each time I walked away from 102 it vanished, only to return as I walked back. Was it in my imagination? Or was it some kind of imprint from the past? A remnant of the vast amounts of coal smoke that spewed into the sky?

~

In the late autumn of 2012, we had been in the North-East to inter Sid's ashes in the same grave as his mum and his brother. ('Three in a bed – a lovely bit of stacking.') The grave is in a far corner of a wind-blasted cemetery in Woodhorn, in the lee of a bramble hedge. We were all there with our partners, kids, my auntie Iris and my cousin Regan. It was another cold wet day, and Nick's partner Wendy, confined to a wheelchair with a broken ankle, was sinking slowly into the turf.

Someone had left a hole for the urn. We put it in. Irene said a few words: 'When Martha and Derrick lived together, they squabbled so much Sid had to play peacekeeper, so it's a good thing he's doing that now.' But soon the cemetery owner was there. He insisted on saying a few words from a book to commit Sid to the soil, as if our laughing and joking was disrespectful. He obviously didn't know Sid.

Then we realized there wasn't enough soil to fill the hole. Where had it gone? The owner went and got some more, and my brothers-in-law Ian and Richard started to tramp down the dirt. So much for solemnity.

Then, in time-honoured Waddell fashion, we went and had a bloody good drink.

∼

People often ask me, 'What's your favourite line of your dad's?' I never really knew until he died. I had many. But since his death one stands out. In 1996, at the Circus Tavern in Purfleet, John Gwynne was musing on what a treat it might be to see Phil Taylor play Eric Bristow in his pomp, a dream made reality the following year.

Sid took the chance to run with this image.

'Maybe, John, there's a darts Valhalla? So we all end up in the sky some time, sitting sipping mead and watching the great ghosts. Might happen.'

Might happen?

I hope it does happen.

Index

Aitken, Jonathan 72
Alamir-Davaloo, Javad 100
alcohol and darts 183–4, 195–8,
    204–5
Allen, Dave 235
Allen, Ted 48
Allix, Dick 218–19, 222, 249, 255
Amatt, Mike 168
Amis, Kingsley 38, 39
Anderson, Bob 181, 182
Anderson, Gary 196
Anglia Television 221
Atkinson, Barry 116
Atkinson, Don 65
Atkinson, Rowan 146
Auf Wiedersehen, Pet 121–2

Banks-Smith, Nancy 190
Banville, John 191
Barneveld, Raymond van 243, 246
Bassey, Shirley 179
Baverstock, Donald 71–2, 74–5, 88, 99
    memoirs 113–14
    Terra Firma 111–12
BBC 111, 113, 193, 209, 230, 231
    British Professional Championship
        203

Grandstand 117–18, 119
Jossy's Giants 167–9
Lakeside World Championship
    242
makes Sid redundant 220–1
1980 World Professional Darts
    Championship Final 144–6
Not the Nine O'Clock News 146
The Prince of Dartness 109–11
Red Alert 249–50
Sid voice-tests for 118–19
Sid's internship at 59
Sloggers 169
starts televising darts 116–18,
    143
Tonight 50–1
and the WDC 221–2
The Wednesday Play 52
Beaton, Steve 223
Bedroll Bella 78–82
Bedside Darts 194
Belle Isle Working Men's Club 91
Bellow, Saul, *Henderson the Rain
    King* 191
Benaud, Richie 236–7, 241
Bernard, Jeffrey 112
Best of Order 76

Boilermaker's Union (United Society of Boilermakers, Blacksmiths, Shipbuilders & Structural Workers) 48–9, 59
Bough, Frank 119
Bowling Old Lane 228
Boycott, Geoff 236
Bramley, Dick 155
St John's 38, 40, 41
Bray, Russ 239
Briggs, Simon 167, 168
World Professional Darts Championship 180, 181, 183, 195
Bristow, Eric 205–7, 218, 239, 257
1978 World Professional Darts Championship 116, 126
1979 World Professional Darts Championship 141
1980 World Professional Darts Championship 144–6
1981 World Professional Darts Championship 147
1983 World Professional Darts Championship 148–53
1985 World Professional Darts Championship 159–63, 173, 174
1986 World Professional Darts Championship 181
1987 World Professional Darts Championship 197
1997 WDC World Darts Championship 243, 272
Sid's commentaries on 190–1
and the World Darts Council 220, 222
British Darts Organisation (BDO) 115, 141, 160, 243
alcohol and darts 196
BDO Opens 248

Lakeside 179–85
1994 BDO World Darts Championship 227, 232–3
and the Professional Darts Players Association 219
and the WDC 217–18, 221–7, 234, 242–3, 248
British Intercounty darts final (1977) 118
British Professional Championship 203
Broad, Chris 236
Bromley, John 88
Brown, Tim 116
Burnett, Richie 243
Burrows, Kevin 225

Calendar 66, 71–4, 89, 100
Cambridge University 32, 34–45
Campbell, Speedy 85–6
Champion, John 38
Chaplin, Patrick 157
Charlton, Bobby 97
Charlton, Jackie 97
Churwell Lions 165–7
Clayre, Alasdair 111
Clemence, Ray 56
Clement, Dick 121
Clough, Brian 97–8
Coates, Phil 37
Cockcroft, Barry 62, 98
Calendar 62, 72, 73, 74
Cockroft, Irene see Waddell, Irene
Cockroft, Nick (Sid's stepson) 21, 204, 209, 217
fish curry 186–8
Irene's relationship with Sid 102, 105, 106, 107
Sid's death 269
World Professional Darts Championship 180, 181, 182

Coleman, David 136, 141
Colley, Ray 109, 111
Collins, Bobby 165
Collins, Patrick 141
Coombe, John 38
Courcey, Roger De 179
Coventry, Harry 161–2
Cox, Tommy 224, 249
   Premier League 255
   and the WDC 222–3
Crawley, John 177–8
Cricket, Jimmy 180
Croft, Lorna 220
Croft, Olly 90, 115, 133, 195, 218, 220
Cunningham, William 133

Dalglish, Kenny 145
Damms, Richard 198–200
Daniels, Conrad 128
Darts World 129, 133, 192
Davidson, Jim 179
Davis, Steve 'Romford Slim' 157, 250,
   252
Dawson, Les 76
Dedicoat, Alan 249
Deller, Keith 148–53, 199, 220
Dodd, Ken 76
The Don of Elland Road 97–9
Donnelly, Dougie 208, 222
Donnelly, Mike 65
Druett, Geoff 66
Durham 48–51
Durham Miners' Gala 66–8
Dyke, Celia 140
Dyke, Greg 204

Embassy World Professional Darts
   Championship 218, 219, 242–4
   Lakeside 179–85
   1978 World Championship 115–16,
      126–33, 139

1979 World Championship 139–41
1980 World Championship 144–7
1981 World Championship 147
1983 World Championship 148–53
1985 World Championship 159–63,
   173, 174
1986 World Championship 181–3
1987 World Championship 195,
   197
1989 World Championship 245
1993 World Championship 221,
   223, 225–6
   origins 114–16
Evans, Alan 86, 115, 147
   documentary on 109–11, 118
   The Indoor League 90–1
   News of the World tournament 87
   Treble Top Championship 117
   World Professional Darts
      Championship 116, 126, 128,
      130, 141
Evans, Chris 249
Evans, Harold 59

Fairley, John 72, 73, 90, 99
Farsley Celtic 177
Fitzmaurice, Martin (Fatzmaurice)
   144, 145, 200
Flaxton Boys 75–6
Fox, Liz 66, 72
Fox, Paul 99
Freeman, Glen 159–63
   Grandstand 172–4
   snooker 197–8
   World Professional Darts
      Championship 170–5, 180–1,
      185
Fry, Stephen 254–6

Garnett, Tony 52
George, Bobby 143, 144–6, 147, 227

Gibson, Barbara 118
Gibson, Brian 66, 73
Glazier, Alan 128, 147, 181
Gower, David 236
Grade, Lew 74–5
Granada 71, 74
    Scene at 6.30 59, 62
Grandstand 117–18, 119, 149, 172,
    173–4
Gravyboatmen 49–51
Gray, Eddie 165
Greater London Darts Organisation
    90
Green, Robbie 197
Green, Tony 136, 200, 210, 245
    as co-commentator with Sid 129,
        132–3, 161–2, 182, 231
    game with Jocky Wilson 142–3
    1983 World Professional Darts
        Championship 150
    split screen television 129
Gregory, Mike 208, 225
Greig, Tony 237
Grumbleweeds 180, 232
Gubba, Tony 173, 174
Gutteridge, Reg 116
Gwynne, John 272–3

Haines, Joe 67–8
Hall, Charles E. 155
    Gravyboatmen 49–51
Harrington, Rod 255, 256
Hearn, Barry 248–9
Heart of the Midlands 116, 128
Hemingway, Ernest 148
Hickling, Dennis 'Bimbo' 236
Hill, Jacqueline 137–8
Hinsley, Harry 39, 40, 44
Holroyd, Lindsey *see* Waddell,
    Lindsey
Hoole, Chris 37

Hopcraft, Arthur 97
Hopkins, Rory 193
Hopper, Terry 60
Howard the Duck 22
Humble, John 138
Hume, David 42
Hunter, Nick 117, 131, 197
    opinion of Sid 126, 140, 193
    Roots of England 118
    split screens 129

The Indoor League 84–92, 115, 118,
    126, 205, 220, 250
Irani, Ronnie 177–8
Ironside, Graham 73
It's A Celebrity Knockout 193
ITV 58–9, 143
    Granada 71, 74
    Scene at 6.30 59, 62
    stops televising darts 203–4
    World of Sport 87–8, 92, 116, 203

Jackson, Ray 65
Jenkins, Simon 192
Johns, Chris 225
Johnson, Colin 144
Jollees Cabaret Club 130, 139, 152,
    159–64, 173, 174, 179–80
Jones, Peter 88
Jones, Tom 179
Jossy's Giants 167–9

K8 Killers 38
Karnehm, Jack 197
Kelman, James, *How Late It Was,
    How Late* 191–2
Kenny, Kevin 208
Khomeini, Ayatollah 140
Kilbourn, Oliver 23–4
King, Mervyn 243, 255
Kirby, Tom 225

La Frenais, Ian 121
Labour Party 67–8
Lada Classic 221
Lakeland, Ray 129
Lakeside 179–85, 201, 204, 205, 226, 242, 250–1
The Landau Lads 111
Langworth, Brian 115
Lanning, Dave 253–4
  friendship with Sid 100, 118, 154, 155, 226, 240
  The Indoor League 87–8, 89
  Lowe's nine-dart 245
  World Matchplay 231
  World of Sport 116
Lazarenko, Cliff 142, 147, 203, 236
Lea, Timothy 79
Lee, Dave 251
Leeds Irish Centre 91
Leeds United 165
Lethbridge, Nemone 111–12
Lim, Paul 245
Little, Ralf 169
Liverpool FC 56–7
Loach, Ken 52
Lord, Stefan 116
Lowe, John 147, 239
  biography 194
  cabaret 208
  Derbyshire Times 114–15
  first televised nine-dart (1984) 245
  1978 World Professional Darts Championship 115–16, 132, 139
  1979 World Professional Darts Championship 139
  1983 World Professional Darts Championship 149
  1985 World Professional Darts Championship 173, 174
  1987 World Professional Darts Championship 195, 197
  1993 World Professional Darts Championship 223
  1995 WDC World Darts Championship 243
  Professional Darts Players Association 218
  Treble Top Championship (1977) 117
  World Darts Council 220
Lowe, Ted 197
Lynemouth 13–17, 211–12, 215–16, 270–1

McGarvey, Danny 59
Macklin, Keith 90
Maori Volcanic Showband 180
Mardle, Wayne 266
Mason, Chris 245
Meade, John (JB) 84, 92, 155
Merseyside Darts Organisation 208
Millar, David 42
Miller, John 131
Miners' Institute (Tute), Lynemouth 15–16
Mitchell, Austin 72
Moore, Brian 116
Morgan, Cliff 209
Motley, James 255

Nail, Jimmy 122
National Iran Radio and Television (NIRT) 99–100
Neuberger, Rabbi Julia 192
News of the World tournament 110
Nolan Sisters 180
Nookie the Bear 179
North Eastern Arts Association 52
Norvelle, Duncan 181, 232
Not the Nine O'Clock News 146

O'Connor, Jimmy 112
O'Dea, Terry 172
O'Reilly, Allen F. 192–3
Ovens, Denis 236

Packer, Kerry 217, 227
Parkinson, Michael 59, 62
Part, John 227, 246, 247
Peck, Tom 250
Phillips, Ken 118–19
Pipe, Justin 196
Pitmen Painters 23–4
Potter, Bob 179, 180, 205, 242
Potter, Dennis 52
Premier League 254–5, 264
Priestley, Dennis 220, 244
The Prince of Dartness 109–11
Private Eye 193–4
Professional Darts Corporation
    (PDC) 217, 234, 235, 242
  Phil Taylor 244–5
  Grand Prix 233
  tournaments 248–9
  2003 World Championship 253
  see also World Darts Council
    (WDC)
Professional Darts Players
    Association 218–19
the Professor 156–7
Pudsey Panthers 167–8
Pudsey St Lawrence 177

Rampage 180
Ramsey, Sir Alf 97
Reaney, Paul 98
Reardon, Ray 149, 150
Red Alert 249–50
Rees, Leighton 115, 147, 199, 200
  1976 *News of the World* tournament
    110
  1978 World Professional Darts

Championship 116, 130, 131–2,
  139
1979 World Professional Darts
  Championship 139
Revie, Don 97–9, 165
Richard, Cliff 180
Robson, Bryan 168
Roddam, Franc 121
Rooney, Wayne 19
Roots of England 118, 131

St John's College, Cambridge
  University 32, 34–45
Samson Classic 223
Scene at 6.30 59, 62
the Schism 217–27, 234
Scott, Mike 59
Scott, Walter 75
Semple, Bobby 116
Shepherd, Alison 198
Sherrin, Ned 112
Sherry 201–2
Sinclair-Scott, Mark 91
Skol 225
Sky 193, 248
  1993 World Professional Darts
    Championship 225–6
  1994 World Matchplay 230–2
  Phil Taylor 244–6
  Sid joins 230–2, 234, 244–7, 250–2,
    265
  Stephen Fry 255
Sloggers 169
Smith, Mary-Jane
  character 24, 25
  marriage to Samuel Smith 61
  religion 25–6, 35, 60, 61
Smith, Rab 116
Smith, Samuel 26, 61
Snowball, Babs 28
Snowball, Jack 28

Index

South Bank Sporting Club 51
Special Correspondent (NIRT) 100
Spendley, Bruce 205
Stafford, Ritchie 209
Stephinson, Ken 67–8
Stirk, Tim 38, 40
Stoddart, Graeme 225
Strickland, Earl 'the Pearl' 250–1
Stump Cross Caverns 69
Summers, Kenny 190
Sutcliffe, Peter 135–8
Sweeney, Walter 'Sonny' 165–6

Taylor, Phil 208, 249, 272
  autobiography 246–7
  nine-dart finish 244–6
  1995 WDC World Darts
    Championship 243–4
  1999 World Matchplay 245–6
  Premier League 255, 256, 265
  talent 148, 244, 253
  World Darts Council 220
Terra Firma 111–12
Thompson, Bobby 122–3
Tonight (BBC) 50–1
Treble Top Championship (1977)
  117–18
Trueman, Fred 85, 91
  The Indoor League 89, 90
Tyne Tees 64–8, 74, 223
  Samson Classic 222–4
  Waddell's World 221

Unipart British Professional
  Championship (1987) 198–200

Vine, David 117, 119–20, 196
  1978 World Professional Darts
    Championship 127, 128, 130
  split screens 129
Virachkul, Nicky 116

Virgo, John 181

Waddell, Bob (Sid's father) 14, 16, 17,
  112, 271
  breakdown of Sid's first marriage
    101
  character 24, 25, 26–8
  death 211–12, 258
  marriage to Martha Smith 60–1
  Miners' Institute 15–16
  mining 23–4, 29
  pitmatic 27
  Pitmen Painters 23–4
  Sid's academic success 28–9, 31, 42
  trains Sid as a sprinter 14, 30
  view of alcohol 26, 27
Waddell, Bobby (Sid's grandson) 260
Waddell, Charlotte (Sid's daughter)
  63, 95, 96
  Donald Baverstock 113–14
  early life 104, 106, 107, 108
  family life 170
  parent's separation 100–3
  Sid's death 269
Waddell, Dan (Sid's son)
  Atari Games System 63
  Churwell Lions 165–7
  cricket 176–8, 228
  early life 14–17, 21, 46–7
  Emma's illness and death 259–62
  family holidays 105–8
  family life 170–2
  football 56–7
  granddad's death 211–12
  Grandstand 172–4
  Jossy's Giants 167–8
  Lynemouth 13–17, 100–1, 211–12,
    215–16, 270–1
  Pudsey Panthers 167–8
  relationship with Sid 233–4
  researches family genealogy 60–1

Waddell, Dan (*cont.*)
  Sid's illness and death 266, 267–8
  at Tyne Tees 64–8
  Unipart British Professional
    Championship (1987) 198–200
Waddell, Derrick (Sid's brother) 16,
  208, 209, 261
  alcohol 270, 212–14
  character 29–30
  death 212–14, 259, 272
  early life 31, 36
  father's death 211, 212
  marriage to Iris 24–5, 101, 102
  Mary-Jane Smith 26
  Sid at Cambridge 41, 42–3
Waddell, Dougie (Sid's grandson)
  18–19, 259, 261
Waddell, Emma (Sid's daughter) 83,
  96
  early life 104, 108
  family life 170
  parent's separation 100–3
  Sid's death 269
Waddell, Emma (Sid's daughter-in-
  law) 259, 261
Waddell, Irene (Sid's second wife) 14,
  15, 18
  Donald Baverstock 113
  Emma's illness and death 259,
    261–2
  family holidays 105–6, 107
  home life 93, 94, 95, 96, 104, 144–5,
    157–8, 170, 235–6
  relationship with Sid 101–3
  Sid voice-tests for BBC 118
  Sid's Ayatollah Khomeini comment
    139, 140
  Sid's cancer 264–5
  Sid's death 267, 269, 272
  television 122, 123–4
  work 21

Waddell, Iris (Sid's sister-in-law) 101,
  102, 215, 272
Waddell, Lindsey (Sid's first wife)
  marriage to Sid 21, 59–61, 100, 101,
    103
  Sid at Yorkshire Television 73
Waddell, Lucy (Sid's daughter) 21, 61
  early life 104–5, 106, 108
  marriage ends 262
  parent's separation 100–3
  Sid's death 267, 269
Waddell, Martha (Sid's mother) 14,
  15, 16, 17, 270–1
  Bob's death 211, 212
  breakdown of Sid's first marriage
    101
  character 24, 26–8
  death 214–15, 258, 272
  Derrick's death 213
  marriage Bob Waddell 60–1
  religion 60–1
  Sid's academic success 28–9, 31, 42
  smoking 15, 16–17, 27, 214–15
  view of alcohol 26–7
Waddell, Maya (Sid's step-
  granddaughter) 18
Waddell, Regan (Sid's niece) 215, 272
Waddell, Robbie (Sid's nephew) 101,
  102
  death 215–16, 259
  death of grandparents and father
    211, 213, 214, 215
Waddell, Seema (Sid's daughter-in-
  law) 18
Waddell, Sid
  academic success 28–30, 31–2, 39,
    42
  Alan Evans 118
  alcohol 55–6, 154–8, 238, 241
  at the BBC 118–19, 193, 220–1, 231
  Bedroll Bella 78–82

Index

Bedside Darts 194
books 191–2
cabaret 207–8, 228–9
Calendar 72–4, 100
Cambridge University 32, 34–45
cancer 257–8, 262–8
as creature of the pub 154–8
death 18, 269, 271–2
Derrick's death 213–14
The Don of Elland Road 97–9
driving 54–5, 136
in Durham 48–51
early career 42
early life 23, 25–6, 28
Emma's illness and death 259–62
family life 105–8, 170–2
father's death 212
Flaxton Boys 75–6
food and drink 188–9
friends 155–8
Granada 74
Gravyboatmen 49–51
health 17, 127, 131, 149, 257–8, 262–8
home life 93–6
The Indoor League 84–92, 115, 118, 126, 205, 220, 250
interviews with 34
joins modern world 254
joins Sky 193, 230–2, 234, 244–7, 250–2, 265
Jossy's Giants 167–9
Lynemouth 14–16, 17
marriage to Lindsay 21, 59–61, 100, 101
National Iran Radio and Television (NIRT) 99–100
1978 World Professional Darts Championship 126–33
1979 World Professional Darts Championship 139–41

1980 World Professional Darts Championship 146
1980s commentaries 190–4
1983 World Professional Darts Championship 149–53
1985 World Professional Darts Championship 160–3
pool commentary 250–1, 252
The Prince of Dartness 109–11
Red Alert 249–50
relationship with Dan 233–4
Roots of England 131
rugby 31, 36–7
rules of commentary 235–41
running 14, 30–1
St John's dart team 37–8, 40
Scene at 6.30 58, 59, 62
'the Schism' 217, 219–20, 222, 226–7
shove ha'penny 85, 86–7, 88
and Stephen Fry 254–6
talent at darts 41
as Ted Allen's research assistant 48–9
television 121–5
ten-pin bowling commentary 251
Terra Firma 112
Treble Top Championship (1977) 117–18
Tyne Tees 74
Waddell's World 221
Yorkshire Ripper 135–8
at Yorkshire Television 84–92, 97–9
Waddell, Vinnie (Sid's grandson) 18
Waddell's World 221
Wade, James 265
Walker, Alan 40
Wallace, Les 243
Warriner, Alan 223
Watterson, Carole 114

Watterson, Mike 126, 130
  1977 Treble Top Championship 117
  1978 World Professional Darts
    Championship 114–16
  split screens 129
The Wednesday Play 52
Welch, Raquel 33
Whitcombe, Dave 147, 190
  1985 World Professional Darts
    Championship 159–63
  1986 World Professional Darts
    Championship 181, 182
White, Jimmy 197
Whitehouse, Mary 80
Whiteley, Richard 72
Wilford, John 72, 76, 155
Williams, Freddie 152, 160, 205
Wilson, Bob 119
Wilson, Harold 67, 68
Wilson, Jocky 42, 141–3, 147, 149
  biography 194
  cabaret 208
  does midnight flit 234
  1987 World Professional Darts
    Championship 195
  and the World Darts Council 220,
    222
Wilson, Malvina 142
World Darts Council (WDC) 217–18
  and the BDO 221–7, 234, 242–3,
    248
  formation 220
  Lada Classic 221
  1994 World Matchplay 230–2, 243
  1995 WDC World Darts
    Championship 243–4
  1997 WDC World Darts

    Championship 243–4, 272
  1999 World Matchplay 245–6
  Samson Classic 223
  World Matchplay 230–2, 245–6,
    266
  see also Professional Darts
    Corporation (PDC)
World Darts Federation 218, 225
World Grand Prix 262
World Matchplay 230–2, 245–6, 266
World Professional Darts
  Championship 218, 219, 242–4
  Lakeside 179–85
  1978 World Championship 115–16,
    126–33, 139
  1979 World Championship 139–41
  1980 World Championship 144–7
  1981 World Championship 147
  1983 World Championship 148–53
  1985 World Championship 159–63,
    173, 174
  1986 World Championship 181–3
  1987 World Championship 195,
    197
  1989 World Championship 245
  1993 World Championship 221,
    223, 225–6
  origins 114–16
World Series Cricket 217, 227
World of Sport 87–8, 92, 116, 203
Wych, Jim 252

Yorkshire Ripper 134–8
Yorkshire Television 62, 144
  Calendar 66, 71–4, 89, 100
  The Don of Elland Road 97–9
  Flaxton Boys 75–6